Short Stories with a Sprinkling of Poetry

By
Rosy Gee

"There are only two days in
The year that nothing can be
Done. One is called Yesterday
And the other is called
Tomorrow.
Today is the right day to Love,
Believe, Do and mostly Live."

Dalai Lama

Contents

A Strange Affair

I was curious about Kay. She spends a lot of time alone in that beautiful cottage of theirs. The one that I had my heart set on until she and her handsome businessman husband parachuted in from London and gazumped us. Their only saving grace is that they live there permanently and don't let it out as a holiday home, like so many other houses in Port Wenlock. The village is like a ghost town in winter.

Tom, Kay's husband, is always away on some business trip or other. He jets off around the world for weeks on end sometimes. Or at least it seems that way. Perhaps I have a skewed view of her life. If I'm being completely honest, I am slightly jealous of her. She doesn't work. She doesn't have to. Tom provides very adequately for her and whatever Kay wants, Kay gets. At least that's how it looks to me.

I hate the way she flicks her long, blonde hair and runs her hand through it seductively whenever she speaks to men. She always does it when she talks to Mike but never when she speaks to me. He had noticed it too because when we were in the pub the other day, Simon and Philippa came in and she was all over Simon like a rash. I thought Philippa was going to deck her but she was terribly sweet and just made sure that she sat tightly next to her husband on the leather couch as if proclaiming him. That didn't stop Kay from sitting directly opposite on the other couch and flashing a portion of her beautifully bronzed well-honed thigh. There's no doubting it; she is a very attractive, dare I say it, sexy woman. She oozes the stuff like butter on a hot crumpet. Men just can't resist her.

"Tom off on one of his trips again, Kay?" Simon asked, raising his pint of Doombar and taking a long draught, before waiting for her reply.

"Yes", she purred, elegantly sipping her chilled white wine, "he's in Geneva this week. Trying to broker a deal with the Swiss Government." She said it so matter-of-factly as if everybody did that kind of thing every day of the week. Not so, Kay. Not here in sleepy little Port Wenlock.

Mike and I had just finished a meal in the restaurant and were on our way out. On the walk back to our cottage, Mike confided in me about his friend back at the pub.

"You're not serious? Do you really think Kay would make a move on Simon?" I asked incredulously.

"Michelle," Mike continued firmly. "I don't think he realises how attractive he is to other women. Have you not noticed how women seem to gravitate towards him whenever he's around? He's such an interesting and charismatic guy."

He had a point. I had found myself eyeing Simon up when he and Phillipa had been round for supper or drinks on the terrace. He had a wicked glint in his eye and was a wonderful raconteur. I could definitely see how women would be drawn to him.

"I know that Kay is a terrible flirt," I responded as we made our way along the long, winding grass track leading to our cottage, "but I don't think Simon would succumb to her charms. He and Philippa are as solid as a rock. You've always said that."

"I know but Simon likes to keep an eye on her whenever Tom's away," Mike continued, "he's always checking up on her, but that's just him being kind. I wouldn't want her to read anything into it, he's always been a very generous and kind-hearted man."

As I tried to settle that night, sleep eluded me. Mike's words were rattling around inside my head and I had a heavy feeling in the pit of my stomach.

I woke to the sound of gulls squawking and screeching as they wheeled and arced in the clear blue sky above our cottage. It was going to be another scorcher. More tourists clogging up the car parks and side streets before they traipse off down to the beach with their stripey wind-shields, buckets, spades, kites and cool boxes, usually with several children and an excitable, yappy dog in tow. Thankfully, I can avoid them, working from home.

I started baking speciality celebration cakes when the family-run baker's shop in the village couldn't cope with their orders. The bakery closed the following year when Asda opened a huge out-of-town store up on the main road into the village, but the internet saved me and I still have a regular supply of orders. I love the flexibility of running my own business and sometimes, when I get really busy, Kay comes over to give me a hand. She's very good. Sometimes we have a glass (or two) of wine when we're finished. An early afternoon reward for all our hard work. She's good company. Mike and I seem to have run out of things to talk about. Kay and I have a good old giggle.

I can see Penderyn Cottage from my study, where I do my accounts and admin stuff for my thriving business. When I looked out across our garden, I thought I saw somebody slipping in through the side gate to the garden. It wouldn't have been the postie because she always shoves the mail through the letterbox in the front door. The beautiful sheltered garden to the side of the house was one of the things I adored about the bigger house next door. When Mike and I viewed it with the young estate agent who showed us around last year, she kept talking about the views out to sea and the wonderful aspect. All I could think about was the suntrap at the end of the garden where Mike and I both agreed afterward over a pint at The Lion, that we could easily sunbathe naked there and nobody would see us.

We had all our ducks in a row and had even paid our solicitor the ridiculous retainer that he had requested, and then the bloody Londoners swooped in and stole it from under our noses. There was no way we could match their offer. Mike didn't seem bothered and said it was meant to be, but I was gutted. I had always wanted to live there, ever since we first moved to the Cornish village twelve years ago following my divorce.

I tried to concentrate on my Self-Assessment tax return, which I had been putting off because I hate filling out forms, and after an hour or so the questions and numbers just kept dancing around on the screen in front of me. It was no good. I needed a break. I checked my watch and smiled. I think I'll pop across and invite Kay round for a drink later. Being as it's going to be such a lovely evening. Might as well make the most of the nice weather while it lasts. Our terrace has a stunning view across the bay and is ideal for a relaxing sundowner. The only trouble is that it's near the road and nosey tourists are always gawping in as they amble back, tired and covered in sand, their fractious children and yappy dogs in tow, carting all their paraphernalia back to their people carriers, which will be stifling hot, like ovens, after being parked up all day in the searing heat.

I made sure I entered the wooden side gate to Penderyn Cottage as quietly as I could. I didn't want to alert anybody to my visit. I could hear voices at the end of the garden so I took the path which led behind the potting shed, remembering the young estate agent's excitement as she led us round to the secret place, hidden from view but with a panoramic vista of the ocean and rugged coastline beyond.

I could hear the voices more clearly now as I was getting closer and one was definitely male. I made sure not to make a noise, treading carefully along the old crazy paving footpath. I had butterflies. When I reached the end of the path and the crazing paving opened out onto the small enclosed terrace, I still couldn't see anything because a granite wall obscured my view. That was why it was so perfect for nude sunbathing. I could just make out a higher-pitched voice, which I presumed was Kay's, and a deeper, more monotone voice.

It was no use. I stopped to compose myself. As I hovered near the gap in the wall which led on to the terrace, I caught a glimpse of the bottom half of two sets of legs, one female (tanned and smooth), and the other male (hairy with knobbly-knees). They must have been sitting very close together. I could hear Kay giggling seductively.

I cleared my throat loudly and stepped out onto the tiny terrace overlooking the sea, the grassy bank below steep, with rocky outcrops. Mike didn't know where to put himself. He leaped up and was all discombobulated. Kay put her glass down when she saw me and glanced across. I noticed an empty bottle of wine on a small side table.

Everything happened so quickly. Kay appeared alongside me and the next thing I knew, Mike was plummeting over the steep bank. He must have hit his head on one of the rocky outcrops with an almighty thud because when Kay and I peered over the edge, we heard a splash and could just see a flash of his red tee-shirt as he sunk beneath the surface of the water. We waited. And waited. Nothing. We looked at each other.

Naturally, Kay and I telephoned the coastguard and emergency services and told them what had happened. Mike had lost his footing on the terrace and slipped over. The whole village turned out for his funeral. Everybody was genuinely shocked to learn of his untimely death and horrified at the way he had met his end. He had quite a high alcohol content in his blood, according to the Coroner's report.

"I've always said how bloody dangerous it is up on that cliff-top at Penderyn," Simon said to his wife as they walked arm-in-arm back to the wake at The Lion. "Poor Mike," he said gloomily, raising a pint of Doombar to his lips after toasting his good friend. Philippa was still in shock as she quietly sipped her vodka and tonic.

Villagers can be very kind and generous at times like this and a constant stream of them called into Dolphin Cottage that summer. They offered their condolences and brought home-made meals and stocked up my freezer with them. Some were awkward and didn't know what to say. Others were used to situations of sudden death. Living on a coastline, it wasn't uncommon for fishing boats to go missing out at sea or even a lifeboat once, which lost all its crew in a terrible storm one Christmas.

When all the dust had settled, Kay divorced Tom (on the grounds that he was never at home) and she and I moved into Penderyn Cottage. It's what I had always wanted.

"You will stop flirting with men now, won't you?" I asked sardonically.

"Of course I will, Michelle, darling", Kay purred, running her hand seductively through her long blonde hair, her eyes sparkling in the evening sun. She licked her full, sexy lips lasciviously then bit the corner of her lower lip. She knew that drove me wild.

We would often sit on the secluded terrace at the bottom of our garden enjoying a glass (or two) of wine, just as the sun was cooling and the intense heat of the day had dissipated. "Here's to us!" we would chant as we chinked glasses. Mike was never far from our thoughts as we relaxed and enjoyed our drinks, watching the evening sun bleed across the summer sky.

The Way I Feel Now

Dam-busted waves, a tsunami crashing through my life
Tossing me like a cork on white water, bobbing and buffeting
Sinking in a maelstrom of sadness, slicing my innards
To pulp, grinding me away to nothingness; I am invisible
The way he makes me feel

Worthless. Soulless. Sad. My heart beats no longer inside me
I have died. Long-gone memories of love; to be cared for, truly
cared for
A simple gesture: checking to ask that I'm okay; not used and
abused
Day after day after day without a second glance from him
The way he made me feel

Courage spurred me on and like a warrior, I rose from the ashes
Phoenix-like, rearing my ugly, beautiful head above the waves
Hatred raging through me like a furnace; eyes fixated on
escaping
I ploughed on, day after day after day until finally, I broke free
From the way he made me feel

I started life anew, shared a room in a stranger's house
Taken in, a stray waif, broken and hollow
I was nurtured; she helped to heal the wounds that were
Sore and open from the way he had treated me, day after day
And I began to feel again

Love came unexpectedly; a bolt from the blue struck me down
Lights came on that hadn't been lit in years, my heart danced
and sang
I felt alive, happy, and full of love once again, the life and soul
Of the party that has now become my new life, day after day
after day
That is the way I feel now

A Once Beautiful City – The Futility of War

Carcasses of burnt-out vehicles litter the disembowelled streets of a once beautiful city. Armed men close in, circling like a pack of wolves. The arid desert air is thick with the stench of fear as their cold-blooded stealth floods the streets and alleyways with hatred.

Wizened mothers protect the fruits of their wombs as best they can. Once happily chanting in their kitchens preparing the regional delicacy, Aushak, the time-consuming dish reserved for special occasions, they were content and safe in their homes. Memories of them lovingly preparing the special family meal; the aroma of mint and gandana fade away as another plume of black, acrid smoke chokes their throats and burns their eyes as they struggle for breath. They fight for survival.

It is not their battle but it has become their fight. They are caught in the crossfire, sometimes played out by politicians in boardrooms and other times by soldiers on the ground. Innocent children, wide-eyed with terror, clutch at their mother's Pashtuns, desperate for peace. Normality. The warmth of a father's embrace.

Aalem cowers in a ruined building with his mother and sister. He recalls how he and his brother played Buzkashi, victorious when the goat hit the target. He hears an ear-splitting blast but by the time his brain tells his legs to move, it is too late. His last thoughts were of his beloved Abdul-Azim. And now he has joined him.

His mother and sister cry out. The woman clutches her remaining child to her breast surrendering to the homeland. The futility of war is too much to bear. She prays that their suffering will end and that she will join her husband and two sons and, once again, they will be together as a family.

An aroma of mint and gandana drifts through the air on the other side of the city. The bodies of the mother and child lay on the dusty, scorched earth amid carcasses of burnt-out vehicles, which litter the streets of a once beautiful city.

⸻⸻⸻

The Fortune Teller – A True Story

My brother was killed in a road accident aged twenty and it ripped our family apart.

I was eighteen at the time, newly engaged and still buzzing from the big family bash we had held to celebrate. Aunties and uncles travelled from far and wide, friends and neighbours in the farming community joined us, and my brother was there too. It was a great party with lots of dancing, loud music, fun and laughter. Certainly, a night to remember.

He died five months later. We were completely devastated. Things like that happen to other people, not to us. It was too shocking and tragic to comprehend and take in. We laid him to rest in the quiet cemetery adjoining the tiny church where I was going to be married.

Working in an open-plan office, (not the Google-inspired spaces of today but a former bedroom in a creepy old manor house) back in the 1970s, I came to terms with my grief as best I could. The old house was home to the headquarters of the local Health Authority where I worked in the Administration Department with Delma, Belinda, Eirlys and Marian, who were great workmates and very supportive friends.

One day Marian, our mentor and supervisor, breezed into the light, airy room and said, "Girls! How do you fancy going to see a fortune teller?' She had a broad grin on her immaculately made-up face and her eyes sparkled; she was the epitome of a Personal Assistant at the top of her game. PA to the Chairman and General Manager, she outshone us as mere shorthand typists at the behest of anybody who needed our services in the sprawling labyrinth of offices, consisting of Nursing, Medical, Dental, General Administration, the Ambulance Department (yes, it really was called that back then) and Planning.

Although sceptical, everybody was up for it, Marian having regaled tales of a friend of hers who had been and was told that some amazing things would happen to her. Whether or not they did, we never found out because Marian was too busy organizing the appointment for us to go and see Dilys, who lived in the back of beyond.

The remote Welsh mining village was about half an hour's drive away from our office and so it was agreed that we would all go, although I was quite reluctant, the bonhomie of my friends won me over and an appointment was fixed for the following evening.

I was still living at home with my parents and younger brother and sister on the farm and Mum's reaction when I told her about our office outing was, "Don't believe anything those people tell you. It's all a load of old nonsense."

Dad was even more scathing. "Don't waste your money."

Needless to say, I met up with my pals in the car park of Starling Park House after work the next day and we all bundled into Marian's swanky new Ford Capri, which she had persuaded her husband to let her take to work that day.

As it happens, the rest of us were all engaged to be married. I think it was Eirlys who suggested that we take off our rings to 'test' Dilys's fortune-telling skills. Giggling like schoolgirls, we each removed our solitaire and sapphire and diamond rings and stashed them safely in our purses.

Marian drove like the clappers and we arrived bang on time. It was six o'clock in the evening when we pulled up outside the austere terrace of ex-miners' houses and clambered out full of excitement and expectation.

Each appointment was to last for twenty minutes and so we would easily make it back to The Welsh Guardsman in Carmarthen for a debrief over scampi and chips washed down with half a lager.

Marian volunteered to go first while the rest of us waited nervously in the front room of the small house, seated on old-fashioned chairs covered in gaudy floral material that had seen better days. There was an old wooden clock on the mantle-piece above a real coal fire which had such a loud tick that we all commented and laughed, saying it was to make sure that Dilys didn't overrun her time-slots.

Soon, Marian came out of a door leading off the room and said, "Oh, my God. She was spot on! She told me all about my Dad passing away last year and my Mum's health problems."

The next thing, a small gray-haired lady with beady eyes appeared at the doorway. She was wearing a tweed skirt and a bottle green twinset and pearls. She had a pair of tartan slippers with fur trim on her small, stockinged feet.

"Who's next then?" she asked in her sing-song Welsh accent.

"Rosy, you go next" the others urged.

I followed Dilys through into the small, dark parlour and felt quite nervous.

"Don't be nervous, love. Take a seat. What's your name?"

"Rosy," I managed to whisper as I lowered myself onto an old wooden chair placed in front of a small table covered with a lace tablecloth. Dilys was on the other side of the table laying out Tarot cards with a look of deep concentration on her bird-like face.

"I want you to pick four cards," she said when she had finished.

I leaned forward and did as she told me, selecting four cards randomly from the rows lying face down on the table. Once I had made my selection, I handed them to her.

She turned the cards over and started talking.

"You work with those ladies out there, don't you dear?"

I nodded, unimpressed.

"You all work in a place where men are in uniform. A dark uniform with a very smart hat. And you're engaged to be married. Why did you take off your ring before you came in, dear?"

I felt myself blushing and thought that Marian must have tipped her off.

"There is somebody who wants to give you a rose, a red rose. Somebody very close to you; he wants to tell you he loves you."

I was confused. My fiancé was very much in the land of the living. Who else loves me?

"If you turn around, you can see him. He's here in the room. He wants to give you the rose."

I stared at her, my mouth agape.

Dilys's voice cut through the maelstrom of thoughts that were swirling around in my head.

"He is asking you to tell Mum not to fret and to tell her he is okay."

Big, salty tears were running down my cheeks and I so desperately wanted to turn around and see my big brother, but I couldn't. I just couldn't do it.

I rummaged for a handkerchief in my bag and mopped up my tears. Dilys's voice was reassuring.

"Don't be afraid, dear. He just wants to give you the rose."

I was heartbroken and sobbing, the grief still so raw.

"Oh, dear. He didn't mean to upset you, dear. It's all right, he's gone now."

I thanked her and left.

The loud giggling and banter stopped dead as I opened the door and my friends saw my tear-stained face. They looked as though they had seen a ghost.

The rest of the evening passed in a blur but when we finally debriefed in the pub, it transpired that Dilys had castigated the others about taking their rings off too, Marian assured us that she hadn't breathed a word, and told them about the men in uniform who we all knew was the smartly turned out Chief Ambulance Officer, and his fellow officers, who regularly came to the Health Authority headquarters where we all worked.

It was late by the time I drove home and the farmhouse was in darkness. I crept in, trying not to disturb Penny the sheepdog, and made my way up the creaky stairs. I stopped when I reached the top, flicked the landing light on and waited tentatively outside my parents' bedroom. They always kept the door closed and the only time I ever went inside was to dust and polish every Saturday afternoon.

I listened at the door and knocked gently before turning the big brass knob and gingerly pushing the old, wooden door open.

"Mum" I whispered.

A bedside lamp flicked on in an instant and my mother sat up. She was wearing a turquoise sixties-style nightie with a flouncy lace trim. I think she was already awake.

"What's up, Rosy? Are you okay? What's happened?"

I sat on the edge of the bed next to her and looked at her. She was a broken woman.

"I have a message for you."

I sensed her recoiling.

"Gary asked me to tell you not to fret and that he's okay."

I couldn't carry on telling her the rest about the red rose or anything else because we were both crying our eyes out.

We never spoke about the fortune teller incident at home after that. Dad seemed to want to believe it but Mum seemed a lot more at ease after that night when I woke her up to pass on a message from her dead son.

When I got married at the tiny village church some years later, I made sure that I had roses in my bouquet. I know my brother was there with me that day, in the church, just as he had been that night in Dilys's parlour.

Time

The wildflower butterflied hopscotch of life
Seeping into and strumming every pore; love so raw
Soaring high, addicted to sensations explored
Fluttering, then plummeting to earth, broken

As grains of sand flow like beaded gold through time
Slipping through our fingertips, draining away
Rainbow-arched happiness gilded with laughter
A dichotomy of pain and pleasure, taunting

Our paths were destined to meet and as
We twist and turn our way through life
Meandering this way and that, a lover's hand
Entwined in mine, warm, safe; life-affirming

And nothing else matters, but you
I feel safe and happy; please don't leave me
I want you to stay forever by my side
And you by mine, but one day, it will end

Smiling, innocent, pretty as a picture
Unaware of what the future holds; do any of us?
We will slip away closing our eyes for the very last time
My heart will snap from the pain of losing you

But before we go, let's laugh, skip and dance;
Rejoice in the fullness of our love, our lives
Our achievements, our failures, our regrets
For when we leave, we can never return

Our time will have come and our time will end

Red Flag Warning Day

Busy making pancakes, I hardly registered what the newsreader announced. It was another red flag warning day in Tahoe Valley.

My day started like any other; a busy working Mom, I rallied the troops and watched as lethargy overcame my brood in equal measures. Sam was first to appear and on the cusp of womanhood, she looks awkward in her teenage skin. She is texting furiously on her iPhone. I glower.

"Do you think you can put your phone down long enough to eat breakfast?" I ask, churlishly. Predictably, there is no response but her sideways glance is clearly, "WTF?"

Aden is next on the scene. Several years younger than his eldest sibling, he sits at the long table and quietly pours a bowl of his favorite Choco-Wheats and tucks in voraciously after drowning the puffed wheat in full-fat milk. It's only when he ignores my question about the Chess Club after school that I realize he's wearing headphones and is in a world of his own.

It's 08:10 and Whitney has yet to appear. The youngest of my three, she is the cutest, sweetest little girl. As innocent as the day is long and so loving. I go to see where she is and find her on her bedroom floor surrounded by soft toys and our Golden Retriever, Sable, sitting obediently to one side seemingly listening intently to every word my daughter is saying.

"Do you want to come to school today with me and Sable, Pixie, or is it your turn Hungry Caterpillar?" She is holding the two adorable characters up for Sable to choose from. My heart aches when I stumble upon this sweet scene.

"Hey! Come on, we're gonna be late and if we don't get a move on nobody will be able to go to school." Whitney is in pre-school but calls it school to keep up with her big brother and sister.

Finally, I manage to herd Sam and Aden out to the sidewalk and watch as they climb aboard the big yellow bus. I wave to them both, as I always do, but they never wave back. They have both begged me to stop embarrassing them but I can't help myself.

As I strap Whitney into her car seat and get Sable to lay on the blanket on the back seat next to her, I feel exhausted and I haven't even begun my day at Bright, Rose & Stavinsky. Aaron and I are both Partners at the firm, he is a Senior Partner and on his way to the top. He has a brilliant mind, but he's also a great husband and Dad.

Finally, I launch into my professional day after dropping Whitney at kindergarten, making sure I get the snuggly hug that she always gives me when we part. Charlene, the TA, scoops my youngest up into her arms and I feel a slight pang of jealousy that the young helper will get to spend the next five hours with my little girl. But this is 2021 and life goes on post-pandemic as we all try to make sense of what just happened.

Thankfully, we could afford homeschooling for the kids and between us, Aaron and I managed to keep working, sometimes just from home and other times using the hybrid method. We got through it with the help of family and friends.

Bright, Rose & Stavinsky had the best year ever. Aaron and I would never have dreamed about the dizzy heights we could and did achieve when we were living the Californian dream as young, hopeful teenagers, now both acclaimed lawyers in our own rights.

My Legal Assistant, Stacey, had my day organized beautifully as always. It was late afternoon when she appeared at the glass Board Room door looking very anxious. There were nine other people in the room. I was chairing the meeting and when I managed to catch her eye, I gestured for her to enter.

"What's up, Stacey?"

"Can I speak with you for a moment?" She turned and left the room, waiting for me to follow. It was unusual because she never disturbed me when I was in a meeting.

I closed the Board Room door behind me. Huddled in a corner of the coffee room opposite, I saw Aaron being comforted by a colleague.

"Oh, my God! What happened?"

Aaron looked up when he heard my voice.

"What is it? For God's sake. Somebody tell me what's happening."

Stacey ushered me inside the room and the other staff member left discreetly as she closed the door behind her, leaving me alone with Aaron.

"Is it the kids? What's going on?"

"Honey," he said, holding my arms and looking straight at me. "The fire jumped the highway and the kindergarten was surrounded before the firefighters could even get there."

"What are you saying?!" I demanded.

"It's too early to say, but we think Whitney might have got caught in the blaze."

Pixie had been chosen to go to kindergarten that fateful day with Whitney. Sable, our faithful pet, had perished too, alongside our beautiful daughter.

The funeral was a blur. It was Sam who suggested a wreath in the shape of the Hungry Caterpillar. Whitney would have loved it. The small, white coffin broke a thousand hearts that day, but none were bleeding more than mine.

I haven't been able to go back to work yet. It's too soon. I can't function. I tidy up the house and my Mom and sister drop by regularly to keep an eye on me. I know they mean well, but I have to get through this.

I pour myself another cup of coffee and sit at the countertop, staring out over the beautiful vista that first attracted us to the house all those years ago. The once beautiful forest is now a tinderbox dry ticking time bomb that exploded right on our doorstep.

Part of me wants to move and leave the Valley forever, but the other part of me is waiting for Whitney to give me one last snuggly hug.

The Sands of Time

I had the world at my feet, life spreading before me like an
unfurled rug

Broken teeth and a smashed-up face resulted from a car crash,
aged just 17

My pretty, innocent, and blemish-free face was now littered with
scars; marred

With pain, my brother died; in a flash, he was gone forever, in
unendurable pain

Tragedy kills you inside for a brief moment in time, then you
learn

To be strong and make the most of every day; to keep going,
keep smiling

Learn to love yourself and be there for your family
wholeheartedly

Calming, helping, healing and assisting as best I could, while
working

Full-time in my first-ever job, finding my feet on the career
ladder

I got engaged and plans were made to marry; we scrimped and
saved like mad

Until eventually a deposit was put down on our very first home

and we wed

In a tiny village church with family, neighbours and friends
helping us

To celebrate our union. The smiles on our young,
impressionable faces filled

With hope, love and the innocence of how our lives would
unfold together

Then tragedy struck again as my darling Dad passed away after a
brief illness

Hand in hand my new husband and I dreamed as we built a
home together

Brought a beautiful daughter into the world and then travelled
to the Middle East

We lived our lives to the full, enjoying every moment, exotic
holidays, fun

Until tragedy struck again and my dear Mum died, again after a
short illness

Now, in my own family unit, we experienced the delights of
expatriate life

Pool parties, swimming over the coral reef in the crystal clear
Red sea

Then repatriation and divorce followed, and more sadness and
pain; I kept strong

Kept smiling. Now, happily re-married, I sometimes reflect on
how quickly

My life has flown by, in a flash. So, stop. Look, listen and reflect, enjoy

Every single moment, before it is too late and, like me, you realise

You have less time ahead of you and more behind you. It is a sobering thought

That makes me reflect and enjoy every moment, every day before the lights

Go out on my life, forever.

Summer's Last Hurrah

Blackberry-laden gossamer-spun hedgerows shimmer in the
morning light

Glistening in the late, weak sun rays warming the last remnants
of summer

Autumn unfurls; leaves bronzed, scarlet-yellow and gold,
clinging to branches

Fluttering and skittering across fallen rose-hip pods scattered on
hard asphalt

Mixed with rotting crab apples creating a collage of nature's
mantle

A magnificent abstract painting of earth daubs and nature's
strokes capturing

The perpetual cycle of birth and death; fragile like a dandelion-
clock-of-life

Seasons as predictable as the ebb and flow of the tides of love
and passion

Seeds sown, miracles grown, reaped and perishing as time
passes, rains set in

Saturating the earth which lies dormant through bleak winters
until in spring

The sleeping earth is awakened as the sun warms its soul to the

core

Summer is all too fleeting; exquisite in its serenity and beauty
and I yearn

For those long, lazy, hazy summer days, once more

Distant Shores

Mai had wanted to travel for as long as she could remember. Her tutor was always trying to get her to concentrate instead of daydreaming the whole time.

Collecting shells along the tropical beach where she lived was something she did every day of the year. She would arrange them in pretty patterns, sometimes symmetrical, others random. She loved patterns.

Mama was always cooking, cleaning, or ironing for the rich folk and her Papa scraped a living by tending to their fancy gardens. Mai yearned to stay on the island but she wanted more, much more.

At school, she had loved art, and aged seventeen, she left to fly to the mainland to study Fashion Design. After she qualified, she was taken on by a big fashion house in London. A few years later when she opened her first store on New Bond Street, she couldn't believe what people paid for her designs. She could have bought a house back home for the price of one dress. It seemed wrong to Mai that some people had so much money and others barely had enough to put food on the table. That was life, and she didn't like it or agree with it.

Mai flew her parents over to London as soon as she could convince them that it was safe and they wouldn't get mugged while walking along the streets. She even hired a bodyguard to keep an eye on them from a safe distance. She spent as much time with them as she could during their two-week stay but was busy working on a new collection. She will never forget the look on her parents' faces when she told them about her plans to become a Fashion Designer. It was a mixture of joy and disbelief; could their little girl be that talented?

On the last day of their trip, she paid a final visit to the lawyers and the papers were all signed. She could relax now.

When her parents landed back home on the island they were met at the airport by a limousine and driven to the better part of the island. There they were given the keys to a mansion with stunning views across the bay. They could see the beach where Mai collected seashells every single day.

Mai visited home as often as her busy schedule would allow but at least now she knew that Mama and Papa could rest easy without having to cook, clean, iron, and tend other people's gardens. Now, they had their own cleaner and gardener but of course, they both helped out because that's what they had always done. They made sure to pay their staff well and were very respectful of them.

Everybody on the island knew the story behind the elderly couple whose daughter they watched every day collecting shells along the beach. Then again, it shouldn't have come as too much of a surprise to them. As her Mama and Papa worked long hours, she used her time wisely and worked at creating patterns in the sand, everything was in the detail. That was important. It was all in the detail.

Mai had worked sixteen-hour days, seven days a week and when she was commissioned to sew thousands of seed pearls on a dress, she never wavered. She kept repeating the pattern over and over, hoping and praying that her diligence would pay off. And it did. That was when she got her first big break and had never looked back since.

Mama came to collect her from the beach today; Papa came for her yesterday. She had been collecting shells for nearly six hours. She was almost running out of places to put them on the soft, white sand, into the endless patterns that she created.

"Come on Mai. It's time to come home now." Tears stung the old woman's eyes as she watched the young woman carefully placing shell after shell in row upon row on the beach.

Mama took her daughter's hand. They trudged in silence up the dunes to the old house they still called home and when they got there, Papa had laid the table for supper. Saltfish, plantain, and eggs, Mai's favourite.

"What do you think goes through her mind while she plays on the beach for all those hours?" he asked his wife.

"Who knows, honey. Who knows. I'm damned if she's spoken a word for the past thirty-four years, so whatever's goin' on inside that pretty little head of hers, stays right there, inside her head."

A Perfect Afternoon

Standing square to the ball, I swing my arms up
Hinge my wrists, shift my weight from the left side
Through to my right, bring the club down, following
Through, swinging like a pendulum and chink!
I hit the ball square on and it flies high into the air
I never knew I could hit such a good shot
Awesome! It felt and sounded fantastic

What a great feeling, watching the ball sailing high
Over the field and into the sky, so, so high
A masterclass on how to hit a ball, my golf pro
By my side, nurturing, teaching, and encouraging me
To keep my eye on the ball, relax and move those
Hips to power through the ball but shots like that are rare

It's not just the golf – or learning how to play the game
It's the great outdoors, fields, trees, grass, manicured greens
Being at one with nature instead of being hunched over
A keyboard which I do every single day, writing, working
Making a living with words, typing them, or creating them
But when I am on the golf course I relax and switch off

The physical exertion is great too – it feels like a good workout
Once I've hit ball after ball after ball, chink! chink! chink!
My shoulders, usually hunched and bunched up leaning over
Open up and out, swing after swing, and it feels amazing
To get that tension out into the open and let it fly away
Melting into the beautiful scenery that surrounds me
I am enthralled with my new love for the sport of golf

Misty Water Hollow

Courtney heard the splashing sound and spun around just in time to see a ripple effect spreading out from the middle of the deep, murky water. It was getting dark but she could have sworn she saw a rowing boat moving slowly away from her.

"Toby! Here, boy," she called, but there was no sign of her caramel-colored Golden Retriever.

"Toby!" she called, louder this time, trying to keep the hysteria out of her voice. Instinctively, she pulled her cell phone from her coat pocket and scrolled through her recent phone calls.

"Rick. It's me. Listen, I'm down at the lake and something strange just happened. I think I saw something. Out on the lake."

Rick said he was up at the house, a short walk away, and reassuringly told her that he would come down right away. Courtney decided to retrace her steps to try and find Toby, calling him constantly, but she was getting more and more concerned the longer time went on. The pine needles and other woodland detritus were thick underfoot and made for slow progress. Where the hell was he? It was unlike him to wander off, he was such an obedient dog.

Fall was her favorite time of the year but today, she wished it were high summer. She was spooked by Toby running off and not returning when she called him. Maybe he'd found a rabbit or something. She tried to think of any number of reasons why he hadn't come bounding through the forest towards her, his big, pink tongue lolling out of the side of his mouth and his soft, furry ears flapping as he gamboled along.

She heard branches cracking and swore she saw something in the distance. Somebody or something moving, swinging. She wasn't sure what. She stood perfectly still, her chest rising and falling as she tried not to panic, fear gripping her chest like a vice. Her breathing became labored as she felt her spine-tingling and her feet became rooted to the spot. Perhaps it was kids playing in the woods making a camp or collecting firewood. It was Halloween, so there were bound to be some shenanigans going on in the woods tonight. She thrust her hands deep into her coat pockets and continued calling out.

"Toby! Here, boy!" she bellowed, as loud as she could. "Come on boy, it's time to go. Here, Toby! Good boy!"

She took her cell from her pocket and hit re-dial but there was no reply. Rick's cell went straight to voicemail. Damn. Where the hell was he?

Witches had been known to make these woods their ritual gathering places, where items, animals, and even, so folklore had it, humans were sacrificed in the name of mystical rites. Dusk was turning rapidly into night and Courtney activated the torch on her phone. It was good to see clearly in a beam of light directly ahead of her, but the darkness all around her seemed to swallow her up.

This was crazy; she had lived near the lake since she was a child. She knew every nook and cranny of the shoreline and had spent many happy times swimming in the clear, fresh water over the years. She and Rick often went skinny dipping in the warmer weather, bringing some chilled beers and the small gas stove to cook burgers on. She felt the same about the woods surrounding the lake; old wives' tales about witches had never bothered her. But tonight, she was spooked.

Suddenly, she stopped in her tracks. She could hear splashing again; it must be coming from far out on the lake. She was starting to feel really cold now and pulled the zipper of her quilted coat up tight in an attempt to keep out the chill air. Crazy thoughts were spinning through her mind about what had happened to Toby and she decided to head back up the hill home to try and find Rick. As she took one last look through the trees towards the lake, she noticed lights like a runway, on the small jetty that she and Rick had jumped off so many times over the years.

Rick had been part of the gang of kids who played here every summer vacation. He was the tall, dark, moody one and they had been attracted to each other early on until eventually, what had started out as a teenage romance, blossomed into true love and they had married, both aged just seventeen. That was over fifteen years ago and they were still as happy now as they were back then. The only thing that had clouded their relationship was not being able to have children. The last round of fertility treatment had completely wiped them out financially and they had decided, regrettably, that it would be their last time of trying. They had had their last roll of the dice. Rick had taken it far worse than she had and was severely depressed. He wouldn't consider adoption or fostering; he wanted to have a baby with his childhood sweetheart. Nothing else could come close.

When he and Courtney took over Misty Water Hollow gas station and store, he was happy to work all the hours God sent. Recently, things had slowed down, real slow and money was tighter than ever. He had even allowed Courtney to take a part-time job at the local school where she had got involved in counseling troubled teenagers. One teenage boy, in particular, had been having a rough time and Courtney had befriended him to help him through a difficult situation. She really shouldn't have left her laptop open with confidential information for Rick to see.

Before they had taken over the gas station and store after his Dad died, Rick and Courtney both worked separate jobs, she as a health care practitioner and he as a truck driver. Their joint incomes had been sufficient but when Rick's Mom generously handed over the business that she and his Dad had run successfully for many years, he and Courtney had jumped at the chance. They enjoyed working together and made a great team. Rick had never been happier.

"Rick! Is that you?" Courtney hollered, scrabbling down the steep incline grabbing overhanging branches as she went, trying to keep her balance as she made her way through the trees toward the lake. He was still a romantic fool and sometimes he would light candles and place them all along the sides of the short, wooden jetty. Recently, he added scattered rose petals for their fifteenth wedding anniversary, culminating in a mouth-watering barbecue with steak, ice-cold beers, and a mountain of chocolate for dessert. They had sat for hours wrapped in a blanket watching the still waters, hearing the occasional splash or ripple from afar, listening to the Coyotes barking and the owls hooting. It was a magical place, a special place; it was *their* place.

As Courtney reached the bottom of the steep slope and made her way tentatively towards the jetty, her torch died. "Damn!" Trying her best to re-activate it, she gave up and slid the phone back into her coat pocket and decided to head to the jetty to grab one of the lights. She stumbled a couple of times in the darkness and could only just make out the lake ahead of her, its eerie dark grey surface taunting her, tempting her to slip into it so that it could wrap itself around her as it had done so many times before. There was a mist rising from parts of the foggy waters and she called out into the dank, darkness once more, "Rick! Where are you?!" desperately trying to keep the hysteria from her voice.

The force of the blow knocked her clean off her feet and she fell forward straight into the lake. Panicking, she kicked and thrashed around, dazed, confused, cold and frightened. Then she felt a pair of strong arms wrap around her, squeezing her tightly.

"Thank God!" she thought, Rick had found her at last. She stopped thrashing around and felt safe in his arms, as she always did. But instead of rising towards the surface as she had expected, she was being dragged further and further from the shore and deeper and deeper down into the icy water. Her lungs were burning and she desperately wanted to scream out, "Help! Help!" but she couldn't. She fought with all her might, kicking and flailing her arms with as much strength as she could muster until eventually, she fought no more.

Two days later, police divers recovered the bodies of Rick and Courtney Blakeford, both aged 32. A police spokesman said that foul play was not suspected and it looked like a terrible accident, but the investigation was still ongoing. The couple's pet Golden Retriever was also found, drowned.

In what police believe to be an unrelated incident, a young teenage boy from the local school was found hanged in the woods nearby. Police are treating his death as suicide.

Who is that Woman in the Mirror?

Who is that woman in the mirror?
The one with the crow's feet and wrinkled skin
Greying hair much more prevalent than before
I don't recognize her, who is she?

Not the young, vivacious woman with bright, sparkling eyes
A spring in her step and a world stretching ahead of her
Exploring, traveling, marrying, and becoming a mother
Nurturing her goals, her dreams, her aspirations

What happened to that woman? Is she still here?
Yes, of course, behind the tired eyes and the lined skin
Remains the youthful, fun, (once attractive) lady
Her vigour may have been dampened oh so slightly

But she is still there, smiling, caring, and loving
Still nurturing with her gnarled hands worn from use
Stitching clothes, gardening, cooking, and baking
For her loved ones, the family that she cherishes

Is that woman smiling back at me *really* me?
Where did all those years go, childhood, adolescence, youth?
Flying by like a tornado uprooting the years and flinging them
Violently into the past, untrodden, unspoken

But now, as I slow down and succumb to growing older
I will never give in or give up as long as there is breath in me
For each new day that life brings, brings with it joy and love
All I have ever wanted, needed and been lucky enough to have

The Beauty of Birds

Iridescent feathers fanned in shimmering awe

Strutting regally, parading its fluorescent plumage

A Peacock's fan bursting with colour: royal blue

Deep emerald green and purple hues

Magnificently displayed, unrivalled beauty

Save for the sweet-tasting nectar sucking

Hummingbirds hovering on delicate blooms

Drinking in their elegance and skill

To sustain their motionless; perfection

Equal almost to the Weaver Bird which

Creates a home for its offspring woven

From grasses into a ball suspended from

A tree branch precarious and perfect

Like a Wren builds a mossy dome to lay

Tiny speckled eggs, her pert tail upright

Strident song bursting forth from her tiny bosom

As a Shoveler scoops up aquatic insects

Crustaceans gleaned from sandy estuaries

A Pelican's baggy throat pouch stores fishy prey

And pretty-as-a-picture pale pink flamingos tip-toe

Through lakes dancing in tune with feeding time as

An owl will swoop with open wings talons outstretched
Ready to pounce on unsuspecting vermin at night and
Kestrels who spy their meal from up high in the sky
Plummeting when spotting a vole or mouse to devour
In sharp contrast to the elegance of a Hooper Swan
Paddling its huge black webbed feet underneath its
Virginal white feathers and elegant elongated neck
Majestically gliding on golden waters silently
Observing the wonder, the beauty of birds

The Gardening Club

Today, the cobalt-blue sky makes my heart sing and I notice a pair of Scarlet Macaws sitting in a tree at the end of our garden. They look as though they are talking to each other. I smile and then shift my gaze to the ocean beyond. I love the way the waves keep gently rolling in, day after day, and the timelessness of the view each time I see it. Each day, I see something different. I have good days and not-so-good days. Today is a good day.

I used to be a truck driver, before the accident. I loved the open roads and meeting all kinds of folk while delivering the goods I was carrying. It was a fine job.

My wife, Alyssa, is a teacher in a private preparatory school and I get to spend more time with her than if she worked in an office or did shift work. Since my accident, she is talking about getting a second job but I am not happy about it.

We had only been married for a few weeks when I lost the use of my legs after the truck rolled back and crushed me against a wall. That's a bitter pill for any spouse to swallow, but for a newly married one, it was real tough. She was and still is, amazing. She makes sure I have something prepared for lunch, even though I assure her that I can manage to feed myself. Sometimes, I try to help out by doing some of the household chores, but I find it tiring and I know Alyssa will only scold me when she gets home. I always know I'm in trouble when she wags her finger at me.

My favorite thing to do is make my way down to the garden, along the shingle path (which can be difficult to navigate in a wheelchair) and pick her a bunch of beautiful, brightly colored flowers. Strelitzias are her favorite – she calls them birds of paradise because they look like exotic birds from afar. I love orchids and I think lilies are exquisite. Alyssa says lilies are for funerals but I disagree. Orchids are my favorites. I sometimes sit and study them in the garden; I love the cheetah-spotted throats of some of the varieties and if you look closely, what looks like a tiny bird's head with a beak peaks out from the soft, velvety cerise-pink, white and baby-pink petals. Most people would be surprised by my choice of flower – it's delicate and serene. I love beautiful things. That's why I love Alyssa so much – she is the most beautiful and serene woman I have ever set eyes upon.

We met in London. I was visiting my parents who had emigrated there some years ago and Alyssa was on holiday with a friend of hers, Tamika. I'll never forget the first time I saw her. She was laughing and her whole face lit up. She has a very open, honest face and the most amazing smile. She and Tamika were sitting on a floating restaurant on The Thames and I was walking along The Embankment. I stopped in my tracks and looked across to where they were sitting. I was drawn across the narrow wooden bridge to the converted barge and ordered a coffee. As soon as Tamika got up to go to the ladies, I struck up a conversation with the pretty lady left alone at the table. We bonded the moment we knew we were from the same island.

Since the accident, I feel as though I have let Alyssa down. We had so much going for us but now, I worry that I'm not enough for her.

Today, I'm not having a good day. I am sitting on the porch of our first home looking out at the ocean and wondering why I am bothering to stay alive. After all, I can't walk, run, fetch groceries - I can't even drive a car unless I get one specially adapted, which would cost too much. And I know that Alyssa is desperate to have a baby. I can't do that either. Father a child.

The black clouds roll in from the horizon threatening to engulf me and I don't even hear Alyssa calling out to me in her beautiful sing-song voice. She came home early that day. She wasn't supposed to find me. I had planned it so that Rodney, the guy we hire to help keep the garden tidy, was supposed to show up, but he was late. The next thing I remember is waking up in hospital and Alyssa squeezing my hand and crying. The doctor was cross with me, I could tell. As if I didn't have enough problems to contend with recovering from my accident, I had gone and done irretrievable damage to my kidneys, he said. I wish the tablets had done their job; I couldn't even get that right.

I was ashamed of myself when I saw how upset Alyssa was. She told me she couldn't care less about anything other than having me around. We talked for hours, sitting out on the porch in the warm, sticky air, thick with the scent of jasmin, night after night. Gradually, I regained my confidence and realized what a fool I had been. The love of a good woman should never be taken for granted and I begged my wife's forgiveness.

Family and friends rallied round and we made it through a rough patch, not made any easier by me feeling sorry for myself the whole time. Alyssa was now working two jobs and I was sitting on my butt all day; I had no choice, but surely there was something that I could do? I read books and thought about writing one but soon dismissed that idea. I wanted to do something for my wife, something special, something that would bring us closer together. And then everything fell into place. In my head, at least. Whether I could pull it off was another matter.

I started the island's first Gardening Club. I kept it a secret, at first, from Alyssa but word spread so quickly, it was hard to keep a lid on it. Aunties, uncles, nephews, nieces, and friends from all over the island came to lend a hand and help out by sharing their knowledge and expertise. We have been able to take cuttings, swap ideas and come up with new ones; I'm even thinking of taking a Garden Design course. With so many people coming in and out of my life, I hardly get a moment to sit on my porch and stare out at the ocean for hours on end, as I used to, all those years ago.

"Daddy, what are those birds called, the ones up in the tree?"

"Scarlet Macaws", I tell my little girl, Shereen, whom we adopted two years ago. Today, it's her 5th birthday and our garden is full of people milling around - family, friends, and lots of children. My parents have flown over from London especially.

Shereen is sitting on my lap in my wheelchair and we talk about the Macaws and I tell her all about how, when the birds meet a partner, they stay together for the rest of their lives.

"Just like Mommy and Daddy." She smiles up at me and my heart melts.

"I love you, Daddy," she whispers and snuggles into me.

I look out to the turquoise ocean above all the hubbub below in our garden, squeeze my little girl and hold her tight. Today is a very good day.

The Red Velvet Dress

Doreen folded the exquisite dress neatly and wrapped it lovingly back into the tissue paper before carefully laying it into the beautiful box where she kept it. She had only worn it once for her daughter's graduation ceremony all those years ago. Where had the time gone? She had hoped to wear it again one day, but that day had never come.

Bob had been gone for almost four years now. What would he have thought about the present situation? She wished with all her heart that he were here to talk things through. What was she going to do?

The gold-edged embossed invitation to her daughter's wedding was propped up on the mantlepiece of Doreen's neat and tidy thatched cottage. The wedding was tomorrow at eleven o'clock and the reception was being held in some fancy country house hotel with parkland vistas and doubtless a bill to make your eyes water at the end of it all. She felt obliged to offer a contribution towards the cost, being as she was the mother of the bride, but the rift between her and her only child had been seismic and she hadn't heard back from Annabelle.

When Annabelle had first mentioned Chris, Doreen had never heard her daughter sound so happy. Gradually, Chris's name was dropped into the conversation more and more until eventually, Doreen asked when they would get to meet him. That was when Annabelle dropped the bombshell.

Bob had been shocked but the fact that his daughter was happy was all that mattered. Doreen had felt very differently and refused to meet Annabelle's partner. That was five years ago.

Saturday morning dawned and Doreen hadn't slept a wink. She thought about all the times she had imagined her daughter's wedding day and how it would be a celebration of love and happiness. Bridesmaids and page boys milling around in flouncy dresses and cute outfits; champagne flutes passed around, and hairdressers, make-up artists, and florists fussing over her daughter. But she wasn't a part of this exciting and very special day. Today, as she sat alone in her lounge at home staring into space, a cup and saucer balanced on her knee, she couldn't have imagined ever feeling so sad and lonely. If only Bob were here, she thought, her lips tight and her face taut with anger. Annabelle had gone too far this time.

When the big double doors opened into the Registry Office, Annabelle scanned the guests for a sign of her mother: a snazzy fascinator or an over-the-top expensive hat, but there was nothing.

The first few bars of Canon in D by Pachelbel began, and it was time to embark on the next phase of her life, leaving the old one behind her and starting a new one with Christine. Her Mum would clearly not be a part of her new life. That had been made perfectly clear by her absence.

As the two women faced each other in the oak-panelled Registry Office and the ceremony was about to begin, a commotion at the back of the room caused everybody to turn around and see what all the fuss was about. The huge wooden doors opened and there, in the red velvet dress that she had worn for Annabelle's graduation ceremony, was Doreen. She looked radiant with a beautiful matching fascinator and clutch bag and was even wearing the Lily of the Valley brooch that Annabelle had bought her as a Mother's Day gift when she was a little girl, helped of course, by her Dad with the payment, but Annabelle had chosen it and contributed a share of her pocket money towards it. Her mother had been thrilled.

Doreen smiled at Annabelle from the back of the room and nodded before taking a seat quietly while everybody settled down again after the Registrar had firmly asked all those gathered together to focus on the reason that they were there, which was to celebrate the marriage of Annabelle and Christine.

As the ceremony began, Doreen took out a white cotton handkerchief from her bag and dabbed her eyes. How could she have been so narrow-minded? The only thing that mattered was that Annabelle had found love and from the way that her daughter looked into Christine's eyes, she had never been happier

Christmas Eve

G iant snowflakes drifted down from the leaden sky as Holly drove through the heavy traffic, an eerie light playing tricks on her as she watched, mesmerized by the fluttering flakes as they floated down and settled on the road ahead of her. It was absolutely magical and she felt like she was inside an enormous snow globe.

It was Christmas Eve and shoppers wrapped in thick woolly hats and scarves were scurrying along, laden with bags, boxes, and Christmas cheer. She had never felt happier. She was driving home to her husband, Greg, to spend their first Christmas together in their new home and she had just collected his gift. He would be thrilled with it, she knew. All she had to do was get home safely.

Both sets of parents had taken some convincing that she and Greg wanted to spend their first Christmas together as man and wife alone, just the two of them, but they had had to agree to meet up on Boxing Day for a big family gathering hosted by Pat, Greg's Mum, who had earned the nickname of Mary Berry because of her amazing culinary and hostessing skills.

Chris Rea's '*Driving Home for Christmas*' was playing on the car radio and it seemed the perfect song as Holly manoeuvred the car carefully through the heavy traffic, which had come to a grinding halt. She checked her phone quickly: no missed calls and no messages. Good. She knew that Greg was working late this evening and that fitted in perfectly with her plans. She had never been so excited about Christmas. This one was going to be extra special.

The traffic started moving slowly and she was aware that the roads were slippery as the snow quickly turned to slush. She pulled up at an intersection and waited as the lights turned from amber to red. Traffic seemed to be going in every direction; she hated this junction at the best of times but tonight, it seemed more chaotic than ever. The lights ahead of her changed from red to amber and then green. She put the car into gear and drove off, singing along with Chris Rea, '*I sing this song, to pass the time away. Driving in my car. Driving home for Christmas.*'

As she reached the brow of the hill, out of nowhere, a car came flying toward her. She screamed and slammed her foot down to avoid an impact but the car was travelling at such speed, it caught the back of her car spinning it round and round. There was a deafening bang, the sound of metal on metal, and grinding noises. The car juddered as she desperately tried to gain control of the steering. Then silence as she finally came to a stop.

A loud whimpering sound from the back of the car broke into her dazed thoughts just before she passed out.

Greg laid another log on the open fire and warmed up some mulled wine. Holly would be home soon and he wanted everything to be perfect. He was surprised that she wasn't home by now, but it was Christmas Eve when everybody goes crazy, grabbing last-minute gifts and goodies to put on already groaning shelves. He put some Christmas music on and turned the lights down low. When the doorbell rang, he thought she must have mislaid her key or knowing Holly, was so laden down with thoughtful gifts and last-minute treats that she was unable to rummage in her bag for the key to their new house.

When he opened the door, a policeman was standing where he expected to see his beautiful, happy, smiling wife.

"Mr. Dodd?"

"Yes."

"Can I come inside?" he asked, his voice breaking. He took off his hat and tucked it under his arm.

Greg stepped to one side and let the man in.

"I'm afraid I have some bad news. Your wife has been involved in a road traffic accident and we found your dog in the back of her car."

"What? Oh my God! How is she? Is she OK? We don't have a dog." The shocked look on the handsome young man's face touched the policeman and he asked him to sit down before he fell down. He knew how shock could affect some people knocking them clean off their feet sometimes.

Standing over Greg in a fatherly way, he put his hand on his shoulder. "Your wife was taken by air ambulance to the General Hospital. I think you had better get over there right away. Come on. I'll drive you."

Greg grabbed his coat and the front door key and was about to leave when the policeman kindly suggested that he turn the music off, make sure the fire was safe and turn all the lights out. "You'd be surprised how many…." he began and then thought better of sharing the shocking news of fires started by Christmas tree lights. "Let's get you to your wife."

When they arrived, the policeman made inquiries at the front desk and was informed that Holly was in the Intensive Care Unit. Greg felt like the bottom of his world had dropped out and he was losing grip on reality. How could this be happening? He had to see her.

"Can I speak to a doctor or somebody who knows what's happening? I need to see my wife" he said, his voice rising as he spoke to the elderly receptionist. The policeman had done his best and had had to leave. He pressed a piece of paper into Greg's hand with the name and telephone number of a local vet where his pet was being checked over.

After what seemed like an interminable wait, Greg was shown into a small side room in the ICU ward. A doctor in green scrubs and black Crocs ushered him inside.

'Your wife sustained some serious injuries, Mr. Dodd, but she is stable now so we are hoping for the best, but I must warn you that it's not looking good.' The surgeon's voice faded into the background as Greg processed the heartbreaking news.

"When can I see her?" he asked urgently.

"A nurse will come and find you in a few minutes, once we've settled your wife onto the ward and made her comfortable."

Greg thanked the surgeon, shaking his hand, and sat back down, a turmoil of emotions running through him. He dropped his head into his hands and prayed that Holly would pull through. When he was finally shown through to see her, he was shocked at what he saw. His beautiful wife lay motionless with her eyes closed and wires and tubes snaked in and around her body. A monitor by the

bed was bleeping and a drip was being fed into her. She looked so delicate. Like a porcelain doll.

"Hey!" he said, taking her hand gently, being careful not to dislodge a plastic tube attached to the back of her hand with some white tape.

There was no response. Greg cried. His entire world was falling apart right before him and the woman he loved more than anything in the world was hanging on to life by a thread. The monitor she was hooked up to beeped steadily.

Christmas was put on hold. No turkey roasted, no crackers pulled, no silly hats around the table as folks read out inanely bad jokes. The family rallied around taking it in turns to have Pepe, the Springer Spaniel pup. Greg kept vigil holding Holly's hand on one side of the bed while her Mum sat on the other opposite him. Neither had slept for days and everybody had lost track of time.

Holly's Mum's phone pinged and she took it tiredly from her bag. "Ah, look, Greg. Pepe likes the snow." She handed her phone to him across the bed where her daughter's lifeless body lay and tapped the screen for the video to play.

Greg smiled half-heartedly as the puppy he hadn't yet met yelped and dug his snout into the snow, running around in frenzied circles yapping excitedly and wagging his tail, thrilled to be outside playing in the snow.

He handed the phone back to his mother-in-law who played the video again, more for a distraction than anything else.

'Jan! Look! Did you see that? Her eyes flickered.'

Holly's Mum dropped the phone and took her daughter's hand in hers, lifting it gently from the bed where it lay limp and lifeless. She squeezed it gently once. Holly squeezed back. Then she squeezed it twice. Two squeezes back.

'One for yes, two for no. Holly, can you hear me?'

Tears streamed down Janet's face as her daughter squeezed her hand once. Firmly this time.

'Oh Holly! Thank God! I love you so much,' Greg managed to croak out in between strangled sobs.

Holly opened her eyes and in that moment, Greg knew that she was going to make it.

Janet left the young couple alone as she went to find a nurse. This was turning from the worst Christmas into the best Christmas ever.

Oceans Apart

Lexi presented the fob to the lock on the pontoon gate and was relieved when it opened with a satisfying click and once through, allowed it to close behind her with a loud clang. She walked down the short sloping wooden walkway and onto the pontoon which made a sound like wobbling planks. Boats of all shapes and sizes were moored on either side and a few people were carrying out repairs because she could see tools and rags scattered on the pontoon alongside their boats. She turned right and continued to the far end where 'Majestic' was moored; she was a beautiful boat.

Rudi's head popped up from below deck when he heard her approaching. 'Why didn't you call me? I could have met you at the gate' he said, his voice full of concern. He came to the side of the yacht and took her bags from her as she gingerly handed them over making sure to pull the hull towards her with one hand to avoid the gap being too wide and dropping her rucksack or overnight bag into the sea, then she grabbed hold of the shroud as Rudi had taught her and hauled herself up and onto the side of the boat, hitching her legs, scissor style over the guard rail. Safely aboard, he pulled her towards him and kissed her tenderly on the lips.

'I've missed you,' he said in his suave public school accent.

'I missed you too,' she said smiling up at him. They had only been dating for a few weeks and as much as she wanted the relationship to work, she had her doubts about its future. Her track record in relationships was disastrous. She seemed to meet the wrong guy at the wrong time and things hadn't ever worked out as she had hoped. They had met on Tinder and she was convinced that he had used a film star's photograph but when they met on their first date, he really was as handsome as his profile pic.

'If you don't mind handing those bags down, I can put the wine in the fridge and we can have a glass with our evening meal.' Rudi disappeared below deck and she passed down several heavy Sainsbury's carrier bags to him before carefully climbing down the wooden steps herself and saw him busily loading goods into the fridge, which was a hole in the worktop in the galley with an insulated plastic lining and held several bottles of wine, milk, butter, eggs and some orange juice. He passed her two bottles of red wine and asked her to put them in the bar. She looked at him quizzically before realising that he was messing with her. She lifted the neat wooden rectangle in the top of the wooden dining table which had been folded down into a slim length behind her in the saloon, and stashed the bottles carefully into the wooden, bottle-sized holes before replacing the lid. It was a very neat set-up.

She had no idea about stocking up a boat before going to sea and was ignorant about how long it took to get anywhere due to tides and all the other things you had to take into account when sailing. This was her maiden voyage aboard Rudi's yacht and it had all sounded terribly glamorous when he had told her about his passion for sailing on their first date, but the few times she had been on board, she thought it was rather cramped and not at all as she had imagined. Somebody had once told her that it was like posh camping on water but she wouldn't have gone that far. She was, however, beginning to think that it was jolly hard work and not all that it was cracked up to be.

Rudi had been sailing since he was a kid when his Dad had taken him out on the Solent as a toddler. He had been around boats all his life and it was second nature to him to sail a forty-foot yacht single-handedly. He told Lexi that he was looking forward to teaching her to sail. She had smiled wanly back at him in the romantically lit restaurant and had been very non-committal.

'So, are you looking forward to our first trip out on the ocean?' Rudi broke into her thoughts.

'Erm, yes and no. I'm looking forward to you taking the helm but I'm nervous about sailing. I haven't a clue how it all works.' She was sitting on the navy and lemon upholstered seating in the saloon alongside the galley and ran her hair through her long dark hair.

Rudi's heart skipped a beat. He thought she was the most beautiful woman inside and out. 'You don't have to *do* anything. I'll sail the boat. If I give instructions, just carry them out.'

'You make it sound so simple,' she said, drawing her knees up to her chest, having been careful to follow the dress code laid out by Rudi some time ago. Boat or deck shoes were to be worn at all times, although barefoot was acceptable when they were moored up and she had been careful to leave her shoes up on deck, no suitcases (due to lack of storage space for non-essential items) and definitely, unequivocally, no heels. That had been a sticking point with Lexi; she loved her high heels and tailored suits but there would be none of that on board. Cotton pedal pushers, tee shirts and warm jumpers were the order of the day, which, quite frankly, she was not looking forward to. She prided herself on dressing smartly for work and was adept at transitioning her outfits to go from office to after work with subtle changes like adding a pretty scarf or removing a tailored jacket and replacing it with a lightweight top over her dress or skirt. She was a classy and elegant dresser and had been complimented on it several times by her colleagues.

'Like most things in life, if you know what you're doing, it's fairly straightforward. Don't worry, you'll be fine,' Rudi reassured her.

'If you say so,' she muttered under her breath.

'Why don't you go and relax on the front of the boat and I'll bring you a drink? I've still got a few things to do so I'll join you later.'

Lexi smiled. He always made her feel welcome and comfortable and she didn't feel under any pressure to get involved with boaty things. She liked the way he spoke about the elegant yacht in terms she could understand: front instead of stern, and although he was slowly teaching her the various parts of the boat and their proper names, he didn't push her.

Lying on her brightly coloured beach towel in her bikini on the pointy bit of the yacht, Lexi felt slightly self-conscious as they were still moored up, but apart from a few people working on their boats, there was hardly anybody around. In the distance, she could see dog walkers with their hounds in tow and people wandering around on the marina while across the other side, bars and restaurants with huge parasols set up outside were starting to fill up with lunchtime patrons. It was the perfect day to eat alfresco.

With the scent of coconut in the air from Lexi's suncream, Rudi's hand appeared through a perspex hatch a few feet from her head.

'A drink for the lady.'

Lexi couldn't help smiling. Rudi had delivered her drink from the stern cabin and presented her with a Pimms, complete with a sprig of fresh mint and half a strawberry.

'I could get used to this,' she said, taking the highball glass from him. 'Are you going to join me?'

'Yes, I won't be long. I've just got a few more things to prepare before our journey in the morning.' And then he disappeared again.

Lexi could feel the heat of the warm July sun on her back as she sipped the deliciously refreshing drink. She felt very decadent drinking alcohol at lunchtime and thought about rustling up a sandwich but then decided against it because she didn't want to get in Rudi's way. Despite having been aboard a few times, she had never sailed on 'Majestic' and had always been spoiled by Rudi's attentiveness; he was the perfect host.

Rudi was a widower and didn't talk much about what had happened, other than his wife had died suddenly in tragic circumstances. They had only been married for three years.

As if Rudi had read her mind, about twenty minutes later, he arrived carrying a small wooden tray containing another glass of

Pimms and two plastic picnic plates, on top of which was a selection of triangular sandwiches with two serviettes tucked underneath. He was wearing shorts and nothing else.

'Cucumber or ham?' he asked, offering her the tray. She took the tray from him and placed it on the towel alongside her, leaving plenty of room for him to sit next to her. They chinked glasses and tucked into the delicious sandwiches, which really hit the spot. After Rudi refreshed their glasses and Lexi enjoyed him sensually rubbing more suncream into her back, he suggested they go down to the back cabin. Lexi knew this was code for some afternoon delight and feeling slightly squiffy after the rather strong Pimms, she could think of no better way to spend an afternoon than with Rudi in bed aboard his yacht.

After a delicious afternoon in the sack (and Lexi had absolutely no complaints in that department whatsoever) Rudi suggested they book a table at the rather fancy brasserie on the quay aptly named Quayside.

Lexi and Rudi were from very different backgrounds. He had had everything handed to him on a silver platter, including a top job in his dad's boat-making company. She, on the other hand, had had to fight every step of the way to get what she had. Raised on a council estate, Lexi had worked her way up Chance Hogarth, a PR company, and was in senior management. Although she loved her job she had always hankered after starting her own business but had no idea of what type of business she wanted to go into. Her parents were from very humble backgrounds and her upbringing was a far cry from Rudi's; she had never encountered anybody receiving an inheritance or heard the term Trustafarian and public schools were something she read about in the press. It was a whole new world and secretly, she resented the fact that he had had it so easy. That was why she had serious concerns about the future of their relationship; they were from very different backgrounds, oceans apart, and she wondered if they could make it.

After a romantic evening at the Quayside brasserie, they walked slowly back to the yacht, Rudi checked the mooring ropes thoroughly and locked the hatch as they were swallowed up into the belly of the boat, just the two of them. Despite having enjoyed delicious sex earlier, they made love again. If nothing else, Lexi reflected in a haze of post-coital bliss in the small cabin subtly lit by the light of the moon, the sex was amazing, but she knew that this was only one small part of the many different facets that make up a successful relationship.

The following morning she awoke to the sound of an engine and what sounded like running water. Climbing across Rudi's empty side of the bed, she pulled on an oversized jumper and opened the door out into the galley. The main hatch was open and a fresh breeze filled the saloon and she could hear Rudi busy up on deck. She was desperate for a shower but didn't know how to operate it; Rudi had shown her the pump action loo which was fine, and she decided to have a strip wash in the basin in the tiny heads. After cleaning her teeth and brushing her hair she dressed in some shorts and a warm jumper and felt ready to face the big day ahead for her first full sail to Padstow.

Slipping on her new boat shoes, she poked her head out up on deck and saw Rudi tying fenders to the guard rails and working through an obviously familiar routine of getting the yacht ready to sail. She didn't know whether to go back down below or make herself useful on deck and before she could make a decision, Rudi had already spotted her.

'Morning! Can you open that hatch on the back and get me another fender, please?'

'Sure.' She climbed up on the cockpit seat, careful not to use the huge steering wheel (or helm as Rudi insisted on calling it) to steady herself, and stepped up onto the wooden deck, locating the locker, she pulled out a navy blue fender and closed the hatch before carefully making her way along the side of the boat holding onto the shrouds as Rudi had taught her before handing it across to him.

'Thanks. Now, can you make sure everything is stowed away properly down below for when we set sail?'

By the time all the pre-sailing checks had been carried out and the harbour master was informed by Rudi over the radio of their intended journey, Lexi began to feel very anxious. They had to go through a lock and she was dreading it. Suddenly she wished she could bail and tell Rudi that she had changed her mind. She really wasn't comfortable with what lay ahead.

'Lexi! Come on, it's time to leave. Can you untie that rope from the cleat and make sure you don't drop it in the water.'

Clicking onto autopilot, she did as she was instructed and decided that she had no choice in the matter. She would try to enjoy the trip and if she didn't like it, that would be the end of her and Rudi. She was very trepidatious about the whole thing because she was convinced that she would fall overboard at some point; the guard rails were very flimsy and one wrong step could be disastrous.

'We have to go and fuel up first,' Rudi announced.

'Oh, great,' Lexi thought, full of unease. Her stomach was churning and she realised that she hadn't even had a cup of tea for breakfast.

'If you don't feel comfortable doing anything, Lexi, just say so. Sit there and I'll get us through the lock.'

Lexi sat obediently on the bench seat in the cockpit huddled up wondering why the hell she had agreed to this trip. Rudi had folded the hood back exposing the working part of the boat, much like the hood on a soft top car and with effortless expertise, steered the yacht from its mooring on the pontoon out and round, activating the bow thruster which caused the boat to turn sharply and they were off.

Rudi had taken the Yacht Master's qualification and was hot on keeping his skills up to date and often did refresher courses in various aspects of sailing, including first aid, sea rescue and a marine radio course and exam. It was all part and parcel of who he was and it showed in his handling of the boat single-handedly and Lexi had a new found admiration for him. His lean, tanned body was taut and after re-fuelling, filling the holder tank with fresh water and navigating the lock, they were finally on their way and out on the ocean. It was seven-thirty and the coastline slowly came into focus as an early morning sea mist lifted and the day felt full of promise as the sun pierced through the low cloud casting shafts of light onto the inky blue water ahead of them.

Rudi looked very accomplished behind the helm and fed the gigantic suede wheel expertly through his hands, a few inches this way and that, keeping the boat on course all the while checking the fixed compass in front of him. He was wearing a white tee shirt underneath a smart grey Musto jumper, which matched his shorts, and grey Musto deck shoes. He looked incredibly handsome and very sexy.

It was early evening when they eventually reached Padstow and Rudi had pre-booked a pontoon inside the harbour which meant that they wouldn't have to use the dinghy to get ashore. No wonder high heels were banned; they would have been so impractical and Lexi, although not one to dress down, accepted that boating was synonymous with comfortable, practical clothing.

A corkscrew motion on the way down had almost had her throwing up and when she went below deck to make some cuppa soups for lunch, she had banged her head so hard she saw stars. To top it all, she had slipped going down the wooden ladder into the saloon and hurt her ankle. Hours and hours of a relentless rocking motion, a brisk breeze that played havoc with her hair and only seabirds for company along the way, she really couldn't see what all the fuss was about; they could have driven down in half the time.

Half an hour later, after Rudi had painstakingly moored the boat up and stowed everything neatly away, curling ropes into coils on the deck, they could finally relax. It was a beautiful summer's evening and the quayside was packed with tourists streaming into the town mooching around the shops, bars and restaurants, all in holiday mode.

'You look tired, Lexi. Is everything okay?' Rudi's handsome face was etched with concern.

'There's a lot more to sailing than I thought. We could have driven down in half the time,' she said, regretting it the moment the words were out of her mouth.

'Well, you stay there and I'll get us something to eat.' He looked hurt by her comment.

Lexi's heart sank. She was hoping to go ashore and get her feet on terra firma as she could still feel a rocking motion as she sat in the cockpit, feeling rather like a fish in a goldfish bowl with everybody looking down at her from the quayside. Even though she had hardly done a thing during the journey she felt utterly drained and was relieved to be safely moored up.

'Can't we go for a bite to eat somewhere?' she called down to Rudi. 'There's some lovely places by the look of it.'

Rudi came back up on deck carrying a bottle of white wine in a chiller sleeve and two posh plastic wine glasses. 'Good luck if you want to try booking a table. I know what'll happen, we'll queue for ages to get a drink only to be told that they're either not serving food because they're full to capacity or if we haven't booked, no chance.'

Lexi's face fell. Of course, she should have realised that a popular tourist spot like Padstow would be heaving at this time of the year. Downhearted, she took the glass of wine from him and felt guilty for toasting, 'Happy days' and smiled at him wanly. Easing himself down, Rudi put his arm around her shoulders and pulled her towards him. She could smell his Penhaligons aftershave and felt his muscular body warm and comforting next to her, the closeness of him making her feel safe and protected. When he kissed her slowly and tenderly, she felt the stirrings of arousal and fought them with all her might. She had to admire his stamina; he had been up since the crack of dawn and she knew that if she had capitulated, he would have taken her down to the front cabin and made love to her there and then. Instead, sensing her demureness, he simply said, 'I expect you're hungry. How does salmon risotto sound?'

'Divine,' she responded as he topped up her glass with another generous measure of Viognier and she suddenly felt guilty for not having been more helpful during the course of their long journey and even more so about not cooking the evening meal, but as

Rudi was obviously so at home in the galley, it made sense for him to prepare their evening meal.

Cocooned in a fantastically warm chunky knit sweater and long trousers, Lexi was warming to the boating fraternity. Folks on the next boat across had invited them over for drinks and after their meal, they had enjoyed the hospitality of a Swedish couple who sailed boats for a living. They ran a yacht charter company and told tales of sailing brand-new yachts from one side of the world to the other, commissioned by extremely rich clients who had neither the time nor the inclination to collect them themselves. Lexi couldn't help noticing the Rolex watches they were both wearing and as well as looking incredibly tanned and healthy, they oozed a relaxed and calm confidence that running your own company brings if done successfully, which theirs undoubtedly was.

The week in Padstow flew by. The boat stayed moored up and they hired some bikes and cycled the Camel trail, enjoyed long lazy lunches after leisurely walks in the surrounding countryside and the culmination of the week was a table for two at Rick Stein's seafood restaurant, which Rudi had booked after pulling a few strings with his sailing contacts. Lexi had never enjoyed a week away so much and clearly had a dilemma. Rudi was an amazing guy, there was no doubting that and he was obviously very into her, but she was dreading the journey on 'Majestic' back home.

The following day, moored up in Island Harbour Marina on the Isle of Wight, Rudi was very subdued.

'So, where are we Lexi?' he asked as they sat in his crash pad apartment lounge overlooking the marina.

'What do you mean?'

'Oh, I think you know exactly what I mean. Are we going to make a go of this or is sailing going to get in the way?'

Lexi blushed. She had been well and truly busted. 'It's not for me, Rudi, but I know how much it means to you and I would never ask you to choose between me and sailing.'

'You don't have to,' he said in a very serious tone of voice.

This is what Lexi had been waiting for. At least he was going to make things easier for her because he was going to be the one doing the breaking up and not her. A tornado of emotions swirled around inside her and suddenly she didn't want to lose what they had. She was incredibly happy when she was with Rudi but just not when they were on a boat. She could feel a lump in the back of her throat.

'I could and never would choose between you and boats. Boats are my livelihood and it's how I make my living. When Dad retires, he'll hand the business over to me. It's worth a lot of money and we've both spent many years building it up and Dad's dad before him. So, no, I'm not prepared to give up boats. I love sailing Lexi, but I love you more. It's been the most fantastic week ever and I want to spend the rest of my life with you.'

Lexi was stunned. A wave of relief washed over her and she felt happy and confused at the same time as a whole raft of emotions shot through her. Rudi was the kindest, sweetest, most dependable man she had ever met and they did have something very special between them. But whether they could reach a compromise remained to be seen.

'Well?' Rudi nudged her for an answer.

'I don't know, Rudi. I mean…I want to be with you but I don't want you to resent me because I'm not a born sailor like you.'

Rudi smiled. 'Come here.' He enveloped her in a tight embrace and kissed the top of her head.

'I have an idea. Why don't you join the family business?'

She looked at him stunned.

'Hear me out. With your knowledge in PR and marketing you could handle that side of things and I'll oversee the boat building. We could do with some fresh input on things.'

Lexi looked at him. 'I'll think about it,' she said non-committally. Rudi was satisfied with her answer for the time being and they made love to the hypnotic sound of halyards tinkling against the metal masts of the boats in the marina outside.

Vacant Possession

Richard and Mary had fallen in love with the cottage as soon as they saw it. The estate agent's voice had faded into the background when they had meandered around the spacious rooms which had been tastefully modernised, while leaving the character and integrity of the old building intact.

After looking around the four-bedroomed property, which stood in an acre of grounds, they were both drawn to the spectacular view from the south-facing garden, which looked out across the Mendip Hills. It was perfect.

Both self-employed, there was enough room for them each to have their own office and a guest bedroom for when the family came to stay and there was even scope to extend if they ever felt the need. Richard was a very successful author of children's books and Mary was a graphic designer. They lived in a four-storey house in Cheltenham but wanted a quieter, slower pace of life. That was ten years ago.

This particular weekend, Richard was away in London on one of his promotional tours, when he would be whisked around various locations to sign copies of his illustrated books and talk to excited children and proud Mums.

Mary had stayed at home this time, happily pottering around in the garden for most of the day before enjoying a relaxing soak in a hot bath into which she had dropped some Rosemary and Eucalyptus essential oils. It was September, so the nights were starting to draw in and she thought about lighting the log burner but decided instead to put on an extra thick woolly jumper after her bath.

In the rustic kitchen, she found her Miles Davis playlist on Spotify and played it on the smart speaker, smiling to herself as she did so. Richard hated Alexa and refused to use her. He would rather time an egg by looking at the clock on the cooker than ask Alexa to do it for him, and on the odd occasion when he did instruct her, he would say things like, "Alexa, stop playing music please," even though Mary had told him to say, "Alexa. Off." She pottered around humming to herself as she prepared a light supper of prawn and avocado salad which she ate at the breakfast bar and then made herself a cup of tea before going through to the lounge to immerse herself in her latest project.

She had always been fascinated with history and had tried to find out more about the cottage, which, according to what she had found out, had been almost derelict in the late 1960s when a couple called Edward Harvey Peterson and Winifred Vera Peterson had resurrected it. When she and Richard had first moved in, they had found a box of old documents up in the attic and Mary had them on the floor by her feet. A Conveyance dated the Nineteenth day of July One Thousand Eight Hundred and Seventy-Six was open out on the floor, beside which she was kneeling, reading the beautiful scripted writing which was on a waxy, parchment-like paper that had yellowed over the years. Sometimes the writing was difficult to understand not only because of the excessive use of swirls and squiggles, but the language was very flowery and long-winded. The document was huge when opened fully and described the property, Yew Tree Cottage, Wendell Lane, Somerset in the County of Wessex as being delineated on the plan hatched in red together with the parcel of land edged in green and described easements and covenants which, their solicitor had informed them, were all quite normal and in order and nothing to worry about. At the end of the document, the purchasers had both signed it in the presence of a witness who had added his name, occupation and address. Both signatures had been witnessed by an Amos Ronald Bridges who had put his occupation as 'Gardener and Handyman' and his address as 16 Market Street, Somerset in the county of Wessex, and Mary wondered if he had been responsible for the creatively designed garden, which had, over the years, been lovingly tended and cared for, and was a beautiful collection of lawns, herbaceous borders, rose beds and, tucked away in the far corner, a vegetable patch and an ancient greenhouse. She and Richard had, during their tenure at the property, added a summer house, a herb garden, and a terrace so that they could enjoy the views while eating alfresco during the warmer weather. They both loved being out in the garden which was a riot of colour in the spring and summer and attracted dozens of species of birds ranging from pretty little wrens to the odd pheasant that would wander in and scratch around in the borders.

At about eleven thirty she decided it was time to turn in and went through the routine that she and Richard had done for years: check that the front and back doors were locked, turn the lights off and switch the landing light on before going up the stairs.

As she made her way up the stairs she suddenly felt a presence, as if somebody or something was behind her. Whatever it was settled on her and she could feel the weight of it on her shoulders and the hairs on the back of her neck stood on end. She turned around but there was nobody there. For the first time in ten years, she wondered if the cottage was haunted.

She didn't believe in life after death but believed that spirits come back and try to pass on messages. She fleetingly wondered if Amos was trying to frighten her because she had re-shaped one of his borders or whether she had disturbed some spirits by raking up the past and digging about in the old document box.

Hurriedly, she washed her face, cleaned her teeth, changed into her cotton nightdress and got into bed. She switched off the

bedside lamp and tried to settle down but whatever was on the stairs was in the bedroom. She sensed it standing over her and a tingling sensation rippled through her as the hairs on the back of her neck began to stand on end.

"Get out!" she shouted, "Go to the light, get out, go to the light!"

Nothing happened.

"Go to the light," she repeated, more calmly this time.

Just when she thought she was alone again, the bed started to shake. Gently at first but then it suddenly became violent, causing her to grab the sheets either side to prevent herself from being thrown off the bed as she was being tossed around like a cork in the ocean.

"Go! Go to the light! Get out!" she screamed as she thrashed about.

Suddenly, the bed stopped shaking and she felt something go into her mouth and she consumed whatever it was that had been in the room.

When Richard returned the following day, he was surprised to see the curtains still drawn and immediately sensed that something was wrong. Mary never slept in past nine o'clock and it was gone lunchtime.

"Hello!" he called, dropping his overnight bag by the front door and placing his keys on the hall table. "Mary! I'm home. Where are you?"

He was greeted with silence. Anxiously, he darted from room to room. He noticed the box of ancient deeds and documents that Mary often rooted through on the lounge floor and there was an empty cup and saucer next to it. He went upstairs with trepidation, calling his wife's name as he went. When he reached their bedroom door it was closed and he braced himself for what he might find on the other side. Pushing the door open very slowly, he said, "Mary? Are you okay?"

He was shocked to see the untidy bed, but no sign of his wife. He was confused because if she had gone out, she would have sent him a text and besides, her car was still on the drive.

"Mary!" he shouted out, "Where the hell are you?" He ran through the house, pulling blinds up and drawing curtains in each room as he went.

When he pulled the kitchen blind up, his heart missed a beat. There she was, sitting on the wooden bench out on the terrace.

"Mary! Didn't you hear me calling you?" he asked, miffed that she seemed to be ignoring him as he strode down the garden towards her.

His wife didn't turn around or greet him as she would normally have done when he'd been away and he noticed that she was still wearing her nightdress.

"Mary, what the hell's going on?" he demanded, hands on hips.

Still no response. He was standing right in front of Mary, just a few feet away, but she was just sitting there with a vacant look on her face, looking straight through him staring into the distance.

A Dog's Life

'Humph. Another bloody visitor. It's Sunday. Don't they know I'm having a dog day?'

Rusty deigned to lift his head from the prime spot on the sofa in consternation as a cacophony of voices, shrieks and chaotic clutter festooned the hall as several people fell through the front door of the modernised Victorian house. And then he sniffed another dog. Female. Things were looking up. He stretched languorously and yawned, a great wide creaking yawn and then he shook his head, 'Better go and see what all the fuss is about.'

Padding out to the kitchen he made a beeline for a rather pretty white ball of fluff. Not his type at all but very attractive and rather shy by the look of her. Two young children were petting her but she was non-plussed and so he walked across and touched noses with her as if to say, 'Hey. I'm the owner's dog. Don't go getting any ideas, pal.' Then he mooched off back to his snoozing spot on the sofa in the lounge.

The two kids followed him through and started making a fuss of him, petting his wiry hair and stroking his head, all the while chattering away to each other about stuff that he knew nothing about. Why couldn't they leave him alone? He wasn't a toy. He had feelings and right now his nose had been pushed out of joint by the arrival of a newcomer. He wondered what the reason was for their visit and more importantly, why they had brought their dog with them.

'Olivia! Rupert! Come along now, we have to go.'

And just as quickly as everybody had arrived causing complete and utter chaos, they left. Silence. Save for a soft whimpering which was coming from next door. Unable to restrain his curiosity, Rusty padded out to the huge, open-plan kitchen with light flooding in from the glorious atrium. Tucked in the corner, curled up in a small white ball of fluff was an intruder. An outsider. Another dog encroaching on his territory. What the hell was going on?

'Rusty! Come along, leave Shoopah alone.'

'What kind of a name was that? Precious little thing, I'm sure. And what was *she* wearing in her fur? Was that an actual pink bow? Pathetic.' Rusty strutted past the precious little pooch and was about to return to his favourite spot on the sofa when his owner announced, "Walkies!" to which his ears pricked up.

'Let's see how the precious pooch copes with all that mud down by the river,' he thought gleefully, wagging his tail as leads and harnesses were put in place. 'Wait, what are those?' On her feet,

Shoopah was wearing shoes. Actual pink doggie shoes. Rusty was disgusted. It was ages before they were ready to leave because the precious pooch had to have a very fancy designer doggie coat put on. He couldn't believe it. He had never worn a coat in his life and didn't intend to ever don one. Not that his owner had ever offered him one, come to think of it.

Eventually, the three of them set off and Shoopah trotted snootily ahead while Rusty sniffed and cocked his leg up every lamp post along the way. Everybody who passed them stopped to pet *her* and completely ignored him. Well, he would show them.

When they reached the end of the street and headed towards the river, his owner let him off the lead and this time, instead of walking at heel and behaving himself, he decided to squeeze through a hole in the hedge and run amok. *He* was her favorite, not that little pooch. He had never heard his owner so anxious, "Rusty! Come back here, you naughty boy. Come back at once!"

Rusty ran and ran until eventually, he was in another field far away from his owner. In fact, he was so far away he couldn't hear her calling him anymore. Well, that would teach her for getting another dog. Wasn't he enough for her? Evidently not. What if he never went back? How would she feel then?

He didn't hear the farmer shouting and as soon as he registered that somebody was shouting at him, it was too late. The gunshot

caught him off guard and mid-leap. He was only trying to get his owner's attention and win back her affection. He didn't even notice that there were sheep in the field.

Shoopah didn't know where to look or what to do. There was a hell of a commotion as the farmer approached the lady walking her with a gun under his arm with the barrel broken and still smoking.

"I'm sorry about your dog, but he was chasing my sheep and they're in lamb," he told Felicity in a very gruff and serious voice.

"But he wasn't chasing them! I saw him, he would never have hurt them."

"That's as may be, Missus, but he was frightnin' my flock and they could lose their lambs. I couldn't risk it." She knew the farmer was perfectly within his rights but she thought he had seriously over reacted. She was heartbroken.

As Rusty drew his last breath, he saw Shoopah looking at him with a very awkward and embarrassed stare unable to meet his dying gaze. She looked ridiculous in those bloody pink shoes.

Later that day when her friend Alexandra came round to collect Shoopah, Felicity was distraught.

"I'm so sorry Fliss. I hope Shoopah didn't have anything to do with it. She wasn't involved, was she?"

"Oh, no, she was as good as gold. I just don't know what got into Rusty, running off like that."

"I'm so sorry for your loss. Will you be okay? We have to get going. Come along Shoopah. Thanks a million for looking after her. The dog walker has never called in sick before."

The Orange Grove

Kitty peddled as hard as she could feeling a rush of excitement as she veered off the wide chalky path which ran alongside the Rio Segura, taking the narrow offshoot leading down to the orange groves, eventually coming to a shaky halt and straddling the bicycle to admire the breathtaking view. A backdrop of mountains gave way to acres of arable land, fields planted with artichokes, others with broad beans and others she didn't recognise. In between were olive trees and in the forefront and surrounding her, orange groves. Rows and rows of evenly planted trees laden with fruit.

Pushing her bike, she stopped to pluck an orange that was overhanging the fence, remembering from way back that this was allowed, and propped her bike up before peeling the succulent fruit, savouring the juicy flesh, leaning to one side to avoid the juice dripping onto her white pedal pushers. She was wearing a straw hat to protect her from the fierce heat and a loose, floaty top and was grateful for the thirst-quenching treat which tasted like no other orange she had ever eaten since leaving this special place in 1982. Enjoying the sweet, sunshine-infused flesh of the fruit, Kitty was transported back thirty-five years, when she and Paolo had first met. He had been a student on an exchange visit that was only supposed to last for a year but, like most visitors to Spain, he had fallen in love and found the pull to stay strong. But it wasn't just the country that had won his heart. The youngsters had caught each other's eye while working during the holidays in the orange groves and after working long days, they would while away the sultry evenings on the Plaza del Ayuntamiento, where the ancient church clock tower, its centuries-old façade crumbling and cracked, would watch over them and all the other patrons who sat whiling away the evenings over coffee and brandy in a convivial atmosphere. The clock was famous for being twenty minutes slow and the locals thought it hilarious, like some private joke between them, never sharing it with tourists or *forasteros*. People who didn't belong. Her iPhone rang, jerking her back to the present.

"Hi! How are you?" she asked breezily, seeing Bryan's name come up on the screen with a photo of him looking rather dapper in a dark green fedora. She wedged the phone between her chin and shoulder as she struggled with a tissue trying to wipe her sticky fingers to avoid getting juice all over the screen.

"I'm fine, darling. How are you? How's it all going? Have you managed to track down your Spanish friend yet?"

Kitty winced inwardly as her husband of thirty-two years asked after her in his usual caring and loving way, oblivious to the real reason she had wanted to come back to this pretty little Spanish village.

"Erm, not yet. I'm still getting my bearings," she lied. "How's everything there? Have you put the green bin out yet? Don't forget that Wednesday is recycling day."

"Yes, I followed your notes to the letter and I haven't starved yet. I see the freezer is stuffed to the gills with your home cooking, all neatly labelled and idiot-proof."

Kitty smiled. She knew Bryan was perfectly capable of rustling up a decent meal but had felt guilty for leaving him on his own.

"So, what are you up to?" he continued in his jaunty voice, and Kitty imagined him sitting cross-legged in his favourite chair in the conservatory, The Times newspaper folded up neatly beside him and a mug of coffee by his side.

"Oh, I hired a bike and I'm just cycling through an orange grove. Well, I was, until I stopped to eat an orange and then you rang so now I have terribly sticky fingers. Hang on a minute." Kitty put the phone on speaker and laid it gently in the basket on the front of her bike.

"Carry on talking, darling," she said in a loud voice, "I'm just going to rinse my fingers off with my drinking water," and she fished around in her rucksack for her water container and poured it over her hands, one at a time, and then wiped them on a clean tissue which she took from a small travel pack in her bag.

"Well, I just wanted to hear your voice, that's all. I got your text to say you'd arrived safely but you know me, I'm an old worry wart." Bryan laughed feebly and she could tell that he was missing her.

After taking a sip of the cool water, Kitty packed the pretty container away and picked up her phone to resume the conversation with her husband off speakerphone. When they finished and had said their customary farewells of "Love you. Love you too," she slid her phone into the zipped pocket on the front of her rucksack, slipped the bag onto her back, picked up the bike and carried on with her journey, feeling slightly uncomfortable and just a tad guilty. Villa Aranceto was just over two miles away, according to the instructions Paolo had sent her, and she smiled at the Italian name of his house which translated to *The Orange Grove*.

She didn't know why she had looked him up, but one morning after a particularly fitful night's sleep when Paolo had invaded her dreams yet again, she had felt compelled to lay his ghost to rest and set about tracking him down. Was it possible that she still had feelings for him after all these years? Surely not. She and Bryan had been happy enough, not ecstatic, firework starburst happy, but bumbling along, middle-of-the-road kind of happy and certainly not *unhappy*. But every now and again, Paola would enter her dreams and stir up emotions inside her that had lain dormant for decades. Sometimes, she awoke with an ache in her heart; an ache for him, and a longing to go back to her past.

Youth is a wonderful thing, she reflected, but the trouble was that when you have it in the palm of your hand, you let it slip through like quicksilver allowing it to seep away instead of savouring every single, precious moment. Pedalling as fast as her legs would go, Kitty felt lighter, happier, and more carefree than she had in years and felt like a teenager again, excited at the prospect of seeing Paolo. He was such a handsome young man with dark, brooding eyes and smooth olive skin, and a strong, muscular body with which she had been familiar with every single contour.

Kitty had never been a FaceBook fan and only had an account to keep track of the boys when they had gone on their travels to India or Botswana or wherever there happened to be a humanitarian crisis. They were good sons and had grown into compassionate and caring men, both becoming doctors, Tim studying further to become an Ophthalmic Surgeon and Will trained to be a Nephrologist, specialising in Paediatric Nephrology. They both volunteered in their spare time and took holidays to places most people would avoid, but it was what they both wanted to do, despite Kitty worrying about them catching some awful disease or meeting a grisly end in the backend of nowhere, and she was incredibly proud of them and hoped that they would settle down one day and produce some grandchildren for her and Bryan.

When she had messaged Paolo, having tracked him down through an old mutual university friend on FaceBook, she wasn't sure if he would respond and if he did, how would she react? But as soon as she saw his message, her face lit up and after a wobbly start, they exchanged e-mails and started messaging fairly frequently, the messages becoming more and more intimate, each filling the other in on the years that had slipped between them.

Paolo had married a Spanish lady called Sofia and they didn't have children. Kitty wasn't sure whether they chose not to have them or whether it was because they couldn't have them but she detected a tinge of sadness when he told her. She told him all about her two boys, Bryan and her life in England.

Eventually, after mulling things over in her mind for a long time, Kitty announced to her husband that she was going to Spain to meet up with an old friend. She knew that he wouldn't mind - he was very easy going - and besides, since she had retired at the beginning of the year, she was determined to do all the things she had been putting off because of work. Now that the 'boys' were off her hands, it was time for *her*. To do all those wonderful things she had dreamed of doing when she was constrained by the day-to-day routine of working full-time while juggling a young family and supporting a busy husband.

Villa Aranceto was clearly one of the better houses in the area and had white-washed walls and a beautifully tended garden. Kitty couldn't help thinking how very Paolo it was. He was always a stickler for being neat and tidy, and was one of the many things that she liked about him. She cycled slowly down the track which led to the property and stopped when she reached a wrought iron gate which led to the back of the house and propped her bike up against the wall. Suddenly she was overcome with nerves and wondered what the hell she was doing. Standing by her bike with her rucksack on her back, she felt very foolish. What was she thinking? She was about to get back on her bike when a voice startled her, "Catherine?"

She spun round and there he was. Just as she had imagined him. He had aged, of course, like her. A few wrinkles here and there and his once jet-black hair was now a wonderful silver-grey. His dark, brooding eyes sparkled mischievously and he had kept in good shape. He was wearing navy blue shorts, a pale blue linen shirt, and navy and cream leather deck shoes. He looked relaxed and was very tanned.

"Paolo?" was all she could manage as they stood there, drinking each other in for the first time in almost four decades.

"Bellisimo!" Paolo opened the gate and stretched out his hands which she tentatively took and placed her hands in his. Her heart was racing and in that instant, time fell away, and they were back in the summer of 1982 when Olivia Newton-John's "*Physical*" had been the soundtrack of their lives as they spent long, lazy afternoons in bed, surfacing only to shower and eat before returning to spend the night in each other's arms once more, never seeming to get enough of each other. They had been so in love and as she stood there, holding Paolo's hands, she suddenly felt like that young woman again. So much had happened since they were last together; they both had families and lives that neither of them had been a part of, but at that moment, it was as if they had never been apart.

"You are just as beautiful as ever," Paolo said, taking in every inch of her as he spoke, his voice soft and throaty. Then, noticing her bike propped up against the wall, he said, "Why did you cycle here? I could have come to you."

Kitty looked down and didn't know what to say. When Paolo had told her his wife was going to be away visiting family in Madrid, she was curious to see where he lived. Now that she was here, in his home, the home that he shared with his wife, she wasn't sure that it had been such a good idea after all.

"Come. Let's find some shade. Would you like a drink?" Feeling slightly awkward she let Paolo lead her round to the back of the house where there was some tasteful garden furniture arranged under an enormous beige parasol on a pretty paved terrace which had huge terracotta pots full of dark pink bougainvillea dotted all around. She sat down on one of the cream sofas and slid her rucksack off and put it at her feet and then she took off her hat and ran her fingers through her hair.

"What can I get you to drink? Are you still a fan of dry Martini and soda?"

She laughed. "Goodness, no! I can't think why I drank it back then. Probably because I thought it sounded sophisticated. What are you going to have?" she asked, looking up at him not quite able to believe that he was standing there right in front of her.

"Well, I have a very nice bottle of Rioja. Can I tempt you?"

"Sure, but can I have a glass of water as well, please."

"Certainly, madam," and Paulo made a small bowing motion which made her laugh and he disappeared through some French doors into the belly of the house. It was a beautiful place, rustic and charming with a classy, homely feel. There was a small swimming pool and another seating area further down the neatly mown lawn. Garden birds were chirping in the surrounding trees and suddenly, Kitty felt as though she was intruding into somebody else's life.

Paolo returned with a wooden tray containing a jug of iced water, a bottle of Rioja and four glasses, two water tumblers and two very elegant wine glasses. He poured a glass of water and handed it to her and she took a few sips before placing the glass on a side table next to her. Then he handed her a glass of wine and poured himself one. He sat opposite her so that their knees were almost touching and she could smell his aftershave. He raised his glass, chinking it with hers, "Here's to...what shall we drink to Catherine?" His voice was like velvet and she felt her stomach lurch. Nobody ever called her by her full name but Paulo used to say that he liked the way it rolled off his tongue.

"Let's drink to friendship," she said smiling and taking a sip of the full-bodied red, detecting notes of cherry, plum and vanilla. "Good choice," she said, setting the glass down on the table next to her water.

Paolo was looking at her intently.

"My God I had forgotten how beautiful you are."

Kitty blushed. "I read all about your successful business," she said, changing the subject. "You really did enjoy working in the orange groves!"

"It's been a team effort. I have some great people who work for me and it hasn't been easy but, like any business, if you work hard eventually, the rewards will come. Sofia and I built it up together." He smiled. "Oranges have provided me with a very comfortable living."

He was as modest as ever, Kitty thought.

"What about you? Are you enjoying your retirement?" He sipped his wine while he waited for her answer.

"Well, it's too early to say really. I only stopped working a few weeks ago. Bryan retired some years ago when he sold his commercial landscaping business but he spends most of his time on the golf course. He keeps asking me to take it up but…"

"But what?" Paolo urged.

"Well, I'm not sure it's for me. Besides, I think it's good to have separate hobbies from your partner."

"Well, I guess it depends on whether you enjoy their company enough. My wife and I play Padel twice a week with friends and I think it keeps us young at heart and the exercise is good too."

That smile again which had always melted her and she felt a tiny stab of jealousy at the thought of Paolo and his wife being so close, which was silly and utterly nonsensical, but it stung all the same. Feeling the effects of the wine, she wondered fleetingly what it would be like if they made love. Would the magic still be there?

Paolo topped up her glass and she was so happy, sitting in his garden in a sleepy Spanish village on a hot, sunny afternoon, sharing a bottle of wine in the company of the man she thought she was going to spend the rest of her life with. Tuscany was Paolo's family home and it would have been a toss-up between living in Italy or Spain. She wouldn't have minded either.

After he poured more wine for himself, he looked at her pensively.

"What is it? Are you going to suggest that we re-kindle our relationship?" Kitty teased, sparring with him, just like old times.

But his face was deadly serious. He didn't answer her straight away but looked down into his wine as if looking for inspiration.

"I have cancer. The doctors have told me it's terminal."

Kitty couldn't process the words at first. "Paolo," she said. "I'm so sorry."

"It's not your fault," he said with a crooked smile. "It's a very aggressive brain tumour."

Kitty felt numb. She looked at him more closely this time; he looked a picture of health; tanned, lean and strong. How could it be?

"I didn't want to tell you in a message. Besides, I wanted to see you one last time."

Tears welled up in Kitty's eyes and spilled over, rolling down her cheeks. She quickly wiped them away with her fingers. She couldn't believe what Paolo was telling her. She got up and sat next to him and they held each other close for the longest time, breathing in each other's smell, trying to memorise every tiny detail, their bodies entwined naturally melding into each other just like before, but only this time, their bodies were old, not pliable and flushed with youth. Embers of their past passion burned deep inside them both.

"You know I still love you, Christine," Paolo whispered. "And I will always love you."

"Paolo." She reluctantly disentangled herself from him, taking a tissue from her pocket to wipe away the tears. She looked down at her pretty sandals, "Why didn't you meet me in the Plaza that night before I flew back home to England?"

"I told you in my letters. Eduardo was supposed to come and tell you that there had been a fire in the hostel and the police were questioning everybody and wouldn't let me go."

Kitty looked at him mystified, "What letters? What fire? I never saw Eduardo."

Paolo was shocked. "Oh, my darling. Did you think I wouldn't come to say goodbye? I wrote to you explaining everything. Besides, we agreed we were going to tell our parents and then meet up again. I wanted to marry you and I thought you wanted to be my wife."

"I did", Kitty said. Her face clouded over and she put two and two together; her mother or father must have destroyed his letters. Perhaps Eduardo was in on it too; he had always been jealous of Paolo.

"But I thought you had changed your mind. We were so young and once I got back home and never heard from you, I thought you had found somebody else."

"Catherine. How could you have thought that? I have never loved anybody the way that I loved you. But after so long of not hearing from you, I thought you had changed *your* mind. I called your home four or five times and each time, your father told me

that you wanted nothing more to do with me. What was I to think?"

Now it was Kitty's turn to be shocked. How different her life could have turned out. She remembered looking at the clock in the Plaza and reluctantly leaving, devastated that Paolo hadn't come to wave her off as he had promised.

She sipped her wine and smiled across at the man who had stolen her heart all those years ago. She thought she was going to cry again but managed to bite back the tears.

"Will you have chemotherapy?" she asked softly.

"No, and the doctors have told me that it's too dangerous to operate. So, my wife and I have talked about it and I would rather have a few months of quality time with her than be hooked up to wires and pipes in a hospital. I will stay here with Sofia by my side." He sounded very matter-of-fact about it all and he and his wife had obviously spent a lot of time talking about it.

Kitty didn't know what to say and they moved the conversation on and away from the dark place that neither of them wanted to be in.

It was late evening when Kitty decided it was time for her to leave after Paulo had prepared a wonderful tapas of deep-fried Padron

Peppers, patatas bravas and calamares fritos, which they enjoyed with their wine, and was absolutely delicious. He was a very accomplished chef.

"Catherine, will you come again? Before you go back," he asked earnestly.

"Of course."

They hugged each other tightly.

"Thank you so much for coming. I never thought I would see you again."

Kitty picked up her rucksack and hat. "Goodbye, Paolo."

"Addio mia bella signora." [Goodbye my beautiful lady].

Kitty forced a smile and blew him a kiss while trying to freeze-frame him standing there looking as handsome as he ever had.

After a fitful night's sleep, Kitty got up at dawn and went out to the tiny balcony of the Airbnb which overlooked the Plaza del Ayuntamiento. If only Paolo had been able to come and say goodbye to her, to reassure her that they would spend the rest of their lives together as they had so often talked about. She had been heartbroken and she remembered her mother being cross with her and had called her a 'silly girl' for falling in love and told her that it was nothing more than 'a holiday romance.' Kitty recalled how much it hurt; the pain of not being with Paolo but worse, thinking that what they had shared together had not been real after all. But after meeting him yesterday, she felt an inner calm she hadn't felt in years. It was all finally sinking in.

As soon as she got back home, Kitty sat Bryan down in their conservatory and told him everything. He told her that he had a feeling that her trip to Spain was some kind of pilgrimage to do with her past, but he had let her go because he knew that she would come back to him. She realised what a good husband he was, and had been over the years, always wanting what was best for her and the boys.

A few weeks after Paolo's messages stopped, Kitty found his obituary online which was heart-rending to read. He was, as she knew, a kind and generous man and had been 'a wonderful husband.' He was buried in the cemetery high on the hill overlooking Villa Aranceto.

She would go and visit him again, one day. But only the next time, she would take Bryan with her to the beautiful village of Formentera del Segura.

On the Edge

Every time Amanda drove past the row of reserved parking spaces at the golf club, she had an overwhelming urge to pull into one of them and today the urge was stronger than ever. As she struggled with her inner self she spotted Loretta's brand-new Tesla parked up ahead and could see her friend pulling out various bits of golfing paraphernalia preparing for their game.

The club was busy today and she had to drive around to the back end of the car park where she was loathe to park because wayward balls from the ninth tee had been known to smash into cars parked there and she winced at the thought of anything happening to her beloved sports car.

Tugging her Cube trolley from the passenger footwell, she proceeded to disentangle it from its carrying case and assembled it. Then she heaved her golf bag from the car boot, the clubs clattering as she did so, and seated it on the trolley before snapping the elasticated fasteners securely into place. Then she changed out of her boat shoes and into her golf shoes, put her mobile phone on silent, slipped it into the valuables pocket of her golf bag, locked the car and was ready to go.

"Do you have a scorecard?" Loretta called, striding towards her and pushing her smart trolley in front of her, reminding Amanda of a proud grandmother pushing a pram. She was immaculately turned out in the latest designer golfing gear and today the colour theme was lime green and grey with a very smart co-ordinated visor.

"Yes, thanks. I always keep a few spares. Do you have one?"

Loretta hadn't heard her because she was rummaging around in the numerous pockets of her smart new Ping golf bag looking for something. Amanda smiled and waited patiently while her friend finished sorting herself out before Loretta suddenly strode off briskly saying, "Come on, we'll be late!"

Amanda trotted along behind hurriedly, unzipping one of the long compartments on her bag and fishing out a navy blue visor which she plonked on her head and tried to tuck in stray wisps of hair as she went, but eventually stopped and put it on properly, before walking briskly to catch up with her friend, who was already half-way to the ladies tee. They were strict at the Fernleigh Golf Club; if you were late or missed your tee time, you were in danger of creating a bottleneck, which never went down well, especially with the more mature members of the Club, and your card was marked. Metaphorically, of course, but Loretta and Amanda's scorecards had gone missing before now so they made sure to capture them on their iPhones before handing them in and always played as fast as they could.

Loretta parked her trolley, snapped on the break, pulled out a tee, a brand-new Callaway ball and slid her Ping big bertha from her bag and walked confidently up to the red markers before she bent down and stuck her tee into the soft earth. Settling her ball neatly in place she stood back, stuck her bottom out, gripped her club firmly and whacked the ball, whipping round beautifully, sending it rocketing into the sky and halfway down the fairway.

"Good shot!" Amanda complimented.

"Yes, I'm pleased with that," she responded matter-of-factly before reclaiming her tee and replacing the cover on her big bertha before stashing it neatly back into its compartment in her bag.

Amanda placed her tee between the two red markers, making sure it didn't go beyond them and thus break the rules. Then she settled her Srixon lake ball in place on top of the bright pink tee and went through a similar routine as Loretta: bottom out, boobs together, head down and eyes on the ball. She too had a good swing and sent the ball straight and true, finishing in the classic golfing position with her right foot on its toe and her club behind her back, having gone full circle. She watched as the ball bounced and bobbed along eventually rolling to a stop about ten meters further on than Loretta's, except that hers was in the centre of the fairway and Loretta's had bobbled into some rough grass to the right. Her friend didn't say a word but just strode off in the direction of her ball, eager to get on with the game.

Amanda had met Loretta quite by chance: Loretta had gravitated to the club after she had sold her recruitment company and needed something to fill her days. Amanda had been referred by her GP through a programme called, Keep Fit and Active: Fight Mental Health and for her, golf was her lifeline. She had been battling demons for some years but recently, things had got a lot worse, and she had been so low that Graham had insisted that she go to see her GP. She had told Loretta when they first met in the group lessons that she had always fancied taking up golf but had never got around to it. Now that she was part-time, having cut down to three days a week, it seemed the perfect time to take it up, she had lied.

"Which club would you use?" Loretta shouted over her shoulder as she was striding purposefully along, nearing her ball in the rough.

"I would use a seven iron but it depends on how the ball is sitting," Amanda suggested, feeling a complete fraud for offering the advice because she had only been playing the game for just over a year, the same as her friend.

"Mm. Good call," her companion said, drawing a golf club from her bag and eyeing up the ball as if trying to magic it out of the tuft of grass that it was deeply nestled in. A few practice shots later, one air shot, which Amanda chose not to see, and the ball was thwacked out and back on the fairway a few meters down, slightly ahead of Amanda's tee shot. It wasn't a particularly good shot but Amanda said, "Good recovery" all the same.

Parking her trolly well to the left of her ball, Amanda drew out her No. 4 iron and lined herself up to take her shot. It was still a good two hundred-plus yards to the pin so she went through the drill that Ben had taught them in their group lessons way back last autumn: arm straight, eye on the ball, whip the hip round and smack! She hit the ball cleanly and with a satisfying chink it went sailing through the air as straight as a dye before bouncing and bobbling along the centre of the fairway a good hundred and fifty meters plus.

Loretta remained tight-lipped and was heading towards her ball a short distance away.

"What club did you use for that shot?" she asked, sounding slightly miffed.

"That was my four iron," Amanda replied.

"I don't have a four iron. I think I'll use my hybrid."

"Go for it."

After going through the usual setup procedure: bottom out, boobs together, arm straight, head down, eye on the ball, Loretta swung back, left knee bent, nice arc and dink. She topped the ball which rolled a few feet and stopped.

Amanda flicked the stroke counter on her trolley forward by one. They were marking their cards today to try and get their handicaps down and although she had not counted the air shot earlier, there was no way she was going to overlook that mis-hit.

Steely-eyed and poker-faced, Loretta took up her stance once more and addressed the ball. This time, she sliced it and it ended up under a gorse bush ten yards or so down the fairway.

Amanda felt sorry for her. They had both worked so hard to master the game but it was an ongoing battle and although Amanda had whittled her handicap down from 54 to 37 after handing in a few cards, Loretta was yet to get off the blocks. Amanda was a kind person and did everything she could to encourage her friend and she knew that once she started to chip away at that huge number, it would come down. It had to. They played twice a week without fail in the winter and three or four times a week during the summer.

Amanda was self-employed, having gone freelance when the pandemic hit. It wasn't out of choice: the small firm of solicitors that she worked for had furloughed some staff and gave her the choice of going freelance 'to enable her to take on other work if she so wished.' Amanda had taken that to mean that she was being side-lined and thought it was due to her age. She wasn't ready to be put out to grass just yet. Besides, she loved her work as a Legal Secretary and was convinced that her career was over and she had lost all her confidence. That was when the sleepless nights had begun and she could hear voices in her head. Hot flashes, anxiety attacks and listlessness had kicked in and she just couldn't settle to do anything. Not even watch the TV. She didn't know what to do with herself and was in a terrible state.

"I suppose I'll have to drop a shot," Loretta announced after fishing her ball out from the base of the bush with a club, measuring the club's length from where it had landed and then dropping it from knee height. Amanda clicked the stroke counter forward by one again. This was not turning out to be a good hole for Loretta. Thankfully, this time, she hit the ball square on with a satisfying 'chink' and it flew off in the general direction of the pin and she seemed pleased with her shot.

The two friends chatted amicably in snatched pockets as they made their way around the course and by the time they reached the fourth hole, they seemed to have settled down and scores of

9, 8 and 7 were pencilled in on the scorecard for Loretta and 7, 6 and 5 for Amanda.

As they approached the tee for the fourth hole, they both tensed. This was the worst hole on the course. An asphalt path led to a sunken hollow beyond which was the green. It was only 141 yards but with broom and gorse to the left and right of the path unless you hit a good long, straight tee shot, you were inevitably in trouble with either a lost ball (meaning the addition of two strokes onto your score) or a very tricky shot out of the rough. To cap it all there was a nasty bunker just before the green on the right.

Neither of them was keen to tee off first and since they had been taking turns to tee off, Amanda manned up and squared her shoulders. Over the course of the year or so they had been playing, they had tried various clubs, but she had reverted to her big bertha and prayed that she hit it as well as her last three shots. You would have thought by now that muscle memory would have kicked in and sometimes, miraculously, it did but whenever she was nervous or anxious about a shot, it always went disastrously wrong. She addressed the ball and completely cleared her mind of all thoughts. Wriggling into her position and settling down, she swung her club back, keeping her head down and as still as she could, she hit the ball squarely and cleanly. Hardly daring to look up to follow it, amazingly it was flying through the air, fairly straight, and landed with a thud on the bank at the far end of the hollow and bounced up, up and onto the green. She was ecstatic and relieved in equal measures.

"Well done," Loretta muttered, no doubt wishing she had teed off first because now she had her work cut out. After much consternation, checking her tee height and settling into position, she took a swipe with her big bertha and her ball sailed through the air, landed on the path and then bounced down into the hollow.

"High five!" she said with glee, offering her non-gloved hand to Amanda who happily slapped it mid-air, American style. "Well done!" she said, "I think we've finally cracked it."

The two women set off pushing their trolleys jauntily, both relieved that they didn't have to go rooting around in the spikey broom and gorse, as they had so often in the past, but could get on and play their balls. As usual, Loretta shot off ahead and as Amanda followed behind, she suddenly felt a black cloud settle over her and her heart felt heavy inside her chest like a lead weight. What on earth would she do when she got home? Graham would have his head buried in The Sunday Times, reading it from cover to cover, along with all the supplements which he devoured hungrily. She admired the way he could lose himself for hours on end simply reading; she couldn't settle to read a book or watch a film; she just got all agitated. It was a Sunday so if she tried ringing the boys they wouldn't answer. Tom was probably running an ultra-marathon somewhere and Will was more than likely cycling to the top of Ben Nevis or participating in what she thought were unattainable and completely pointless challenges. But they were both fit and healthy and they never seemed to stop doing crazy things. She wished they would stop sometimes, just for a minute or two, and ring their Mum. She loved to hear their voices.

Loretta brought her back to the present when she shouted from down in the grassy hollow, "Can you believe that?! It's in a rabbit hole!" She picked her ball up and placed it to the side on a flat mossy surface and started to line herself up to pitch the ball up onto the green. She did a pretty good job, hitting it a little too heartily and sending it skipping along to the back of the green where it sat tantalisingly on the brim before rolling down and off the back into the rough.

The round progressed pleasantly and the ladies had good holes and not-so-good holes but that was the nature of golf. Unpredictable, exhilarating, and frustrating in equal measures. It was just gone three when they got back to the car park and reversed the procedure they had carried out on arriving: folding trolleys and packing them away before stowing them in their cars, hoisting their golf bags into their boots and changing back into their everyday shoes.

"Have you got time for a coffee?" Amanda asked Loretta hopefully. She never seemed to have time to do anything except be a slave to her three Cocker Spaniels.

Checking her watch she said, "Okay. Just a quick one," and off they set to the recently refurbished Club House where small groups of golfers sat chatting over beer, coffee, or wine and there was a general ambiance of bonhomie which Amanda liked, although nobody ever came over to them for a chat. She assumed it was because they were still fairly new to the Club and wished she were more outgoing. She used to be so happy-go-lucky but since hitting the menopause, it was as if her spirit had hidden away somewhere deep inside of her. Sometimes she felt like her heart had stopped beating and she was only a shell of her former self.

"I'll get these," Loretta insisted, waving her membership card at the young lad behind the bar and a wonderful smell of roast Sunday lunch permeated the bar area. Amanda found a seat and they settled down with their latte's dissecting the game and berating the fact that they didn't think they would ever get a decent handicap.

"Are you alright," Loretta asked her friend, scrutinising her from the chair opposite.

"Not really. I don't know what's wrong with me, to be honest. I just feel down all the time."

"Have you been to the doctor's?" Loretta asked in her no-nonsense tone of voice.

"Yes. My GP said I was menopausal but I'm past all that. Anyway, she recommended CBT and something called the Silver Cloud programme. Waste of time if you ask me. All meditation and mindfulness nonsense."

"Well, it might be worth taking it more seriously. If it's a specifically tailored programme then it must have benefits for some people. If ever you need to talk, you know I'm here for you."

"Thanks." Amanda smiled and didn't feel as though she could open up to her golfing buddy. Besides, what would she say? *I'm sad. I'm not happy. I feel isolated and alone* but yet she was surrounded by kind, loving family and friends. But none of them seemed to notice her. Not *really* notice her. Except for one. Her friend, Diane, sent her a text every so often asking how she was doing and they would meet up for coffee in Fernleigh, a lovely old market town, and would wander around the shops after their coffee and she had felt much better as if during that brief period of time she was able to leave her demons behind.

"Well, best be off before the dogs wreak havoc. They'll be needing a walk and that's the last thing I want to do now, if I'm honest, but I'll have to take them."

Loretta had never married and didn't have children but she had lived a full and interesting life, starting up her own company and travelling the world recruiting staff for high-net-worth individuals. It all sounded very glamorous to Amanda in comparison to her dull and boring life.

When Loretta got home, she Googled 'menopause' and was astounded at the things she found out about it and how deeply it can affect some women. She was one of the lucky ones, as she had sailed through hers and out the other side without even realising it. She knew that it was a long shot but she felt as though she wanted to do something to help, something meaningful. Once a businesswoman, always a businesswoman, so she set about looking into setting up a foundation and she knew just the person to ask for advice. For the following few days, she researched as much as she could and her plan was beginning to come to fruition.

"Amanda? Are you alright? Where are you? You sound half asleep." Amanda sounded strange when Loretta called her.

Silence.

"Amanda! Where are you?!" Loretta demanded in her headmistress's voice.

"On the coast," came the cryptic reply.

"Where, on the coast?"

"Erm. Somewhere near Barmouth. I think."

"Amanda, what's going on?" her golfing buddy asked.

"I just needed some space, that's all. Some fresh air."

"Have you forgotten we were playing today? I thought it was odd when you hadn't turned up. Listen, I'm going to drive up to wherever it is you are and you can tell me all about it. I'll head for Barmouth and then call you again when I'm getting close. Okay?"

"Sure," Amanda replied, suddenly snapping out of her stupor.

"Right. I'm on my way."

After Loretta cut the call, she sensed that something was very wrong and she did what any friend would do and drove as fast as she could to get to her friend.

In the meantime, Amanda opened her car windows fully and let the fresh sea air fill the car. As she opened the window on her side of the car, the garden hose she had fixed in place fell away and it was as if Loretta had smacked her around the face. 'What in God's name was she thinking?' She threw open the car door and reeled the short length of hose up, removing the other end from the exhaust pipe. She was about to turn the key in the ignition when Loretta's calls had come through, one after the other until Amanda had had no choice but to answer. She stashed the pipe in her boot and hid it under her golf shoe bag as if by hiding it would erase from her memory what she was going to do with it.

She got back into her car and drove from the remote location she had chosen and made her way down into the town of Barmouth, pulling up in a pub car park. She went inside The Ship Inn and ordered herself a large brandy and went outside to find a table. It was a beautiful summer's day; kids were running around on the beach, dogs were yapping as they chased frisbies and young mums cradled babies wearing floppy sunhats.

She managed to find a small table that had just become vacant. A young couple smiled and offered her their table as they left. "Beautiful day, isn't it?" the young man said. "Yes, lovely," was all she could muster in response. Her legs felt weak and her stomach was churning. As she sat down and took a sip of the brandy, her phone rang. It was Tom, her eldest.

"Hey, Mum! How are you?"

"Oh, you know. I'm okay. How about you?"

She wiped the tears that were streaming from her eyes with the back of her hand, desperate to hide the fact that she was crying, but Tom knew better.

"Mum? What's up? Are you okay? What is it? Is it Dad? Talk to me, Mum," he pleaded.

"Honestly, Tom. Erm, I can't really talk now but I'm okay. Really. I have to go. A friend of mine is meeting me for lunch,' she lied, "And she's trying to get through. We'll talk later. I promise," and she ended the call.

Loretta located her friend on the pub terrace and strode straight over to her. Amanda stood up and as the two women hugged she crumpled against her friend and Loretta almost had to hold her up as she folded into her embrace, tears streaming down her face. Wiping her eyes with a tissue Loretta produced from her pocket, Amanda talked and talked while her friend listened. Another double brandy later and she was starting to feel half-human again.

"I'm taking you home to Graham and we'll sort your car out later. I'll speak to the barman to make sure we can leave it there overnight if need be." It was clear why Loretta had been so successful; she took control of the situation and left no stone unturned.

"Come on. Let's get you home and from now on, if you want to talk, call me. Do you hear?"

Amanda nodded and allowed herself to be taken control of because she wasn't capable of thinking clearly herself.

Over the course of the next few months, the two women became firm friends and met regularly in Loretta's uber-smart kitchen, discussing the best way forward with their new business venture. Amanda felt like she had a purpose in life now. Her journey wasn't over but she was making good progress with the help and support of family and friends and she was slowly getting back on track. She had finished the Silver Cloud programme and had taken up meditation and yoga. Out on the golf course, she was making good progress with her handicap too.

"Did you know that if a ball sits on the lip of the cup, you can wait ten seconds and if it falls in before the ten seconds is up, it counts?" Loretta announced when they were on the sixth green. Amanda smiled. That is exactly how she had felt all those months ago; teetering on the edge wanting to fall but desperately trying to hold on and not topple into the abyss.

"Come on", Loretta said, "Those old duffers behind are catching us up," and she strode off purposefully towards her trolley as Amanda trotted along behind trying to catch her up.

Printed in Great Britain
by Amazon